This Little Church Stayed Home

THIS LITTLE
CHURCH
STAYED
HOME

A faithful Church in deceptive times

Dr. Gary E. Gilley

EVANGELICAL PRESS
Faverdale North Industrial Estate, Darlington, DL3 0PH
England

Evangelical Press USA
PO Box 825, Webster, NY 14580

e-mail: sales@evangelicalpress.org

web: http://www.evangelicalpress.org

British Library Cataloguing in Publication Data available

ISBN 0 85234 603 4
ISBN-13 978 0 85234 603 7

All Scripture quotations, unless otherwise indicated, are taken from the New American Standard Bible, copyright © 1960, 1962, 1963, 1968, 1971, 1972, 1973, 1975, 1977 by the Lockman Foundation.

Printed in the United States of America

Contents

Foreword

During the fall of 2004, Pastor Gary Gilley participated in a radio interview on Jan Markell's show, *Understanding the Times*. I was part of that same show — that's how I met Pastor Gilley. After the show I told Jan, 'I think I just met a spiritual twin brother I never knew I had.' Gary's analysis of the condition of the church coincided with my own, and his passion for the integrity of the church and her message resonated with me. I am honoured to commend Gary's latest book to you.

Today, a number of credible people are sounding the warning that the evangelical church has gone seriously off track — only a few of these watchmen, however, are pastors. There are reasons for this. Many pastors have succumbed to the seeker movement and left discernment aside in order to please as many people as possible. Another reason is that pastors pay a price for publicly addressing controversial issues and caring for a congregation is difficult enough in its own right. Furthermore, many pastors are theologically sound and feed their flock the pure Word of God, but they are just not writers or researchers. So when a pastor like Gary Gilley comes along who is willing to help the rest of us understand the most important issues facing the church today, we are blessed.

As a pastor, Gary cares for the welfare of the Lord's flock. He is also part of a small cadre of us who, in addition to pastoring, enjoy the battle of ideas in the arena of public debate. This band believes it is good that ideas are freely debated publicly so that everyone can see what the issues are and follow up with their own search of the Scriptures. Gary balances his providing light on important issues with his passion for the welfare of the church. He couples strong warnings with a heart of love and compassion for those the Lord has bought with his blood.

Some consider it unbiblical to correct error and name the false teachers who trouble the church. Paul didn't. Every one of Paul's epistles corrected errors and false teachings. Several times Paul named false teachers as he warned the church about their heresies.

False teachings are inimical to the welfare of the church. They often come to us as the latest technique for spiritual growth, church growth, or personal enhancement. This was true during Paul's life and beyond when the New Testament was written — it is no less true today. The need is as great today as it ever was to name these errors for what they are and to refute them.

Paul described a necessary attribute for elders: 'Holding fast the faithful word which is in accordance with the teaching, that he may be able both to exhort in sound doctrine and to refute those who contradict' (Titus 1:9, NASB). This is precisely what Gary is doing in *This Little Church Stayed Home*. Many today consider correcting false teaching to be a breach of pastoral ethics rather than a necessary qualification for the faithful discharge of one's pastoral duties. Pastor Gilley follows the biblical pattern and challenges us to not let the 'consensus building' trend of our culture dictate the pattern of the church.

If the evangelical movement is to remain rooted in the fundamentals of God's Word, it must heed the warnings of men like Gary Gilley. If we fail to heed these warnings, we shall find ourselves 'evangelical' in name only. *This Little Church Stayed Home* is a solid book that must be read. Gary is calling us to 'stay home' rather than wander off with the popular trends of the day. I pray that many people read this book and, by God's grace, stay home.

Pastor Bob DeWaay
Twin City Fellowship
Minneapolis, Minnesota

Preface

Tinker Bell was dying. Her little light had all but flickered out and Peter Pan stood helplessly by. What could be done to save Tinker Bell? Peter had no medicine and there was no doctor in the house. But Tinker had an idea: she thought she could get well again if children believed in fairies. Peter immediately cried out to all the dreaming children everywhere, 'Do you believe? If you believe, clap your hands; don't let Tink die.' As the dreaming children all over the world clapped, Tinker Bell revived and was soon as healthy and robust as ever.

Apparently sometimes, at least with imaginary fairies, all that is needed for flourishing health is having enough people believe in you. I wonder if this approach could be adopted by the evangelical church community — or perhaps already has been. If enough Christians believed the church was healthy, maybe she would be. Maybe if we clap loudly, we will make enough noise to give the appearance of being vigorous. Yet despite all the claims of spiritual interest, despite the runaway numerical growth at the celebrated megachurches, despite frequent 'sightings' of revival and despite the rapid succession of fads (from Promise Keepers to the 'Prayer of Jabez' to 'Forty Days of Purpose' to 'The Passion of the Christ'), each promising to reform the church, the fact is the church's light is flickering. Let's start with the obvious — numbers. Megachurches (worship attendance of 2000 or more) are springing up weekly (there were 842 in February 2004), church buildings are rapidly being constructed, Christian concerts and rallies are well attended, and other glowing statistics could be given. However, two recent studies have cast an ominous shadow over this seeming success. George Barna, in an e-mail dated 4 May 2004, informs us that since 1991 there has been a 92% increase in the number of adults in America who do not attend church (from 39 million to 75 million). Then *U. S. News and World Report* in its 19 April 2004 issue stated, 'Surveys confirm that the percentage of Americans attending a weekly worship service fell appreciably during the past four decades. From roughly 40 percent in the 1960s, it today hovers at about a quarter.'[1] Something just does not add up.

Barna, in his attempt to scrutinize this church attendance freefall, candidly writes, 'Unchurched people are not just lazy or uninformed. They are wholly disinterested in church life — often passionately so. Stirring worship music won't attract them because worship isn't even on their radar screen. More comfortable pews cannot compete with the easy chair or the bed that already serve the unchurched person well. Church events cannot effectively compete with what the world has to offer.' This analysis should come as no surprise in light of Scriptures such as Romans 3:11, 'There is none who understands, there is none who seeks for God'; and 1 Corinthians 1:18, 'For the word of the cross is to those who are perishing foolishness, but to us who are being saved it is the power of God.' Why did anyone ever think that unbelievers were going to be attracted to Christ if we could only offer him in an attractive package? The truth is, rather than drawing people to Christ, the gospel message has itself been gutted of its power.

What are the followers of Christ to do? Barna suggests, 'The rapidly swelling numbers of unchurched people may be forcing existing churches to reinvent their core spiritual practices while holding tightly to their core spiritual beliefs. It will take radically new settings and experiences to effectively introduce unchurched individuals to biblical principles and practices.' This strikes me as the same rhetoric that the seeker-sensitive church has been propagating for years. For two decades the church-growth experts have told us that if we are to attract the unchurched, we must change the way we 'do church'. We must offer them new 'settings and experiences'. We must meet their perceived felt-needs. We must do away with biblical exposition and focus on stories. We must eliminate dogma and become relevant. We must do away with hymns and major on contemporary music. We must remove our Christian symbols and traditions and behave more professionally and secularly. We must train our pastors to be CEOs rather than shepherds. When we have done all of this, we have been assured, we will attract the masses. Now, after two decades of church leaders buying and implementing everything that the market-driven gurus have offered, we find far fewer people attending church services (of any kind). Their methodologies have failed, yet Barna encourages us to keep it up. If we can just change enough, if we can just offer the right experiences and become more creative, surely we will ultimately break through.

But this is the wrong approach. The church cannot, as Barna has noted, compete with the world system. We just don't have the money, the people, the expertise. But more importantly we are not offering what the world offers. And this is where we need to concentrate our thinking. The Christian community has something to offer that no one else has: the truth as found in Jesus Christ and the Scriptures. Rather than running about trying to keep up with the world, we need to return to the one thing the world cannot give.

But herein lies a major problem. While the evangelical church has been chasing the ever changing fads and whims of our society, she has jettisoned her unique message. At the same time that the church has forgotten her purpose, she has also been infiltrated by a wide range of diluting and corrupting influences that have changed the very core of her being. In *This Little Church Went to Market,* I identified many of these influences. Others will be identified at this time, but in the milieu of the biblical understanding of the church. I want to discuss what God says a church should be — what it should hold dear and emphasize, what its distinctive should be. All of this will be done in the context of the unique pressures and temptations facing God's people in the twenty-first century. It is not enough to identify what is wrong with the church; we must also offer an alternative — one firmly founded in the timeless Word of God rather than in the trends of tomorrow. If much of the modern church has sold its birthright and gone 'to market', what would a church look like that resisted these trends and 'stayed home'? That is, what would a church be like if it drew its cues from Scripture — if it truly believed that God has a paradigm for the church outlined in his Word? This will be the approach that will be followed in this book.

What do the Scriptures say?

Harvard professor Kirsopp Lake made this insightful observation:

It is a mistake often made by educated persons who happen to have but little knowledge of historical theology, to suppose that fundamentalism is a new and strange form of thought. It is nothing of the kind. It is the partial uneducated survival of a theology which was once universally held by all Christians. How many were there, for instance, in Christian churches in the eighteenth century who doubted the infallible inspiration of all Scripture? A few, perhaps, but very few. No, the fundamentalist may be wrong. I think he is. But it is we who have departed from the tradition, not he, and I am sorry for the fate of anyone who tries to argue with a fundamentalist on the basis of authority. The Bible and the corpus theologicum of the church are on the fundamentalist's side.[2]

Lake, who was writing in the 1920s and represented the emerging liberal wing of Christendom, hit the nail on the head. Fundamentalists (those who adhere to the fundamentals of the faith) had not, and have not, moved. Their final authority continues to be the Scriptures. They attempt to develop their personal lives and local churches according to the instruction and model found in the Bible. The classic liberal, lacking confidence in the Word, marching to the tune of modernity, developed a quasi-Christianity created in the image of man — they have reaped what they sowed. The so-called new paradigm church movement today has not bothered to dispense with the Scriptures. In fact many, if not most, of these churches consider themselves evangelical and would declare that they are believers in the inerrancy of the Bible. The problem is they lack confidence in the Scriptures and have therefore co-mingled it with a plethora of supplemental sources. The effect is that while clinging tenaciously to a doctrinal statement affirming biblical inerrancy, the authority of Scripture has been undermined. Of what real value is a Bible that we cannot trust? If the Bible is not sufficient, as well as inerrant, then it has no real impact in how we live or how we structure the church.

In essence, the new paradigm church, during these last two decades, has done exactly what the liberal church did a hundred years ago — they just have not been honest enough to admit it (or perhaps are ignorant of what they have done). Both groups have replaced Scripture with the wisdom of their age. Instead of evaluating every thought and movement of society by the Word, they have pressed the Scriptures through the grid of modern thought. That portion of the Word which survives this process can be embraced; the portion that does not can be ignored. Few are so bold as to say this out loud, leading to much confusion and deception, but this is the spiritual landscape in which the twenty-first century church navigates. This is the mindset of the vast majority of evangelicals.

Of course, this approach cannot be tolerated by the lover of God's Word. Such lovers of the Word have resisted the siren call of the age, and have not wrecked their lives and churches on the rocky shores of the latest fad or philosophy. Why is this so? What makes the difference? It is too simple to say that one loves the Word and one does not — both may adore the Bible and its Author. The difference, it seems to me, is the place of origin. One begins with God's Word, developing his theology, philosophy for living and worldview from the Scriptures. These believers are then able to filter, with discernment, whatever the world or the Christian community is throwing at them. The other begins with trends, fads, prevailing philosophies, demographic studies, surveys, and pragmatism, squeezing scriptural truth into this quagmire where possible. With this approach, while retaining the handle of 'evangelical', the philosophical tail of secular thought and opinion, wags the biblical dog. Scripture becomes subservient to faddish opinion. The Christian and church that desires to stand firm against the pressures and distortion all around them must begin with Scripture. They must develop their worldview and ecclesiology from the Word before they look at a survey or demographic study. Before they are tempted to incorporate Eastern mysticism prayer techniques, or integrate psychological principles, or change worship services to please the seeker, they must first discover what God says. Upon that immoveable bedrock of what God says — and wants — they can build both their lives and churches, and evaluate the whirlwind of ideas swirling around them.

So, we will begin with the Scriptures. As we do so, we want first to identify the marks of the true church. What does God say the church should be and do? Then we will juxtapose these marks with the strong trends that are challenging them as found in evangelical Christianity at this present time.

In the infant days of the church, as outlined in the book of Acts, we find a newly regenerated people, with no money, no buildings and no program having an astounding impact on their world in a very short time. As the newly born church began, what was important to them?

1) Evangelism (2:41, 47)
2) Worship (2:46-47)
3) Prayer (2:42)
4) Truth (2:42)
5) The ordinances: baptism(2:41) and communion (2:42).
6) Purity (5:1-6)

I believe we will find these same marks of the church repeatedly presented as foundational throughout the epistles. If we must pick one of these marks to begin our study, I believe it needs to be the mark of truth. Truth must exist. Truth must be knowable. Knowable truth must have a source. Although there are certain things that can be known through general revelation (Ps. 19:1-6) the primary and only infallible source for truth is the Word of God (Ps. 19:7-14). On these things most who would call themselves evangelical Christians, we would assume, would agree — although as we will see this is a faulty assumption.

Nevertheless, since it is the biblical position, we are not surprised to find Paul informing us that 'the church of the living God [is] the pillar and support of the truth' (1 Tim. 3:15b). Whatever else the church of God does, it must excel at undergirding and proclaiming the truth. I believe a local church can fail at many things, but it must not fail at holding forth the truth of the living God. To fail at this is to fail at the primary mission given to the church. The church is not free to create truth, to supplement truth, to alter truth, or to selectively obey truth. The church is 'to exhort in sound doctrine and to refute those who contradict' (Titus 1:9). The church is to 'contend earnestly for the faith which was once for all delivered to the saints' (Jude 1:3). The church is to 'preach the word; be ready, in season, and out of season; reprove, rebuke, exhort, with great patience and instruction' (2 Tim. 4:2). To not accept these commands as a sacred trust is to totally miss the most important reason for the church's existence. But as we will see in the chapters that follow, the twenty-first century, engulfed as it is in postmodernism, is not an environment in which truth can easily flourish.

A Postmodern World

1

An Historical Overview

A pastor, in criticism of my stubborn insistence that the first priority of the church is to be the 'pillar and support of the truth', wrote, 'The Bible does not place a great priority on being right. We are to be holy and righteous, pure and just. We are to believe, understand and proclaim the truth. But that is not the same as being right.' Welcome to the world of postmodernism, where words don't mean what they mean, truth is subjective and contradictions in logic are perfectly acceptable. Until we understand that our philosophical climate in the Western world has changed, we are going to be both frustrated and confused attempting to fulfil the truth mandate as given to the church (1 Tim. 3:15). It is therefore of vital importance that we understand the times in which we live.

The changing times

We must begin with a broad overview of history and a look at the three philosophical and religious eras that have dominated Western civilization.

Premodern

During the premodern era, which extended from medieval times until the French Revolution of 1789, the Western world believed in the supernatural. No one doubted the existence of God (or gods).

Spirits, demons and other beings existed beyond the realm of the senses; and this spiritual world somehow controlled and dominated life in the physical world. Of course there were many worldviews thriving under premodernism. Animism, mythology, Greek philosophy and Christianity all flourished and battled during the premodern era, but as diverse as they were all held firmly to a belief in some form of a supernatural spirit-world.

Biblical Christianity is obviously premodern in this sense. When presenting the gospel it was not necessary to convince people that spiritual beings or gods existed — everyone believed this. The challenge was to persuade individuals that there was only one true God, who sent his Son into the world as the God-man to die for their sins. In many ways the premodern worldview (which still exists in numerous places throughout the world) was a more fertile environment for the spread of the gospel than either modernism or postmodernism. One of the criticisms levelled at Christianity during the last three centuries is that since it is steeped in premodernity it is primitive and foolish. The supernatural carries no regard in modern thought; therefore, the supernatural had to be jettisoned by the liberal church to gain respectability in Western society. But we are getting ahead of ourselves.

Modernism

The foundations of premodernism began to shake a bit with the arrival of first the Renaissance and then the Reformation, but it was the Enlightenment that proved to be its undoing. Influential philosophers such as Immanuel Kant (1724-1804) began questioning not only the dogmas of the past but also all sources of authority. By this time the Western world's authority was to be found primarily either in the church (Roman Catholicism) or in the Scriptures (Protestantism), or in the case of Islam in the Koran. The architects of the Enlightenment challenged these authorities, including the beliefs founded upon them, and offered in their place human reasoning. 'The goal of the "Enlightenment project" … was to free humanity from superstition and found a philosophy and civilization on rational inquiry, empirical evidence and scientific discovery. The term "modernism" is often identified with this overall project. The modernist vision presupposed the power of rationality to discover truth.'[1]

The Enlightenment would usher in the age of modernity. Michael Kruger writes, 'With the rise of the Enlightenment there came a new guardian of truth to replace the church: science. No longer would human beings stand for the irrational musings and archaic dogmatism of religion — science (with reason as the foundation) was the new god, and all intellectual theories had to bow and pay homage in order to be seriously considered. Science viewed Christians as being naively committed to ancient myths, unable to see past their bias and to take an objective and neutral look at the world. So modernity proffers the idea that mankind, armed with rationalism and science, is able to access absolute truth and make unlimited progress toward a better life for itself. Therefore, at its core, modernity is a celebration of human autonomy.'[2] Deism would emerge for those wishing to be both enlightened and religious. The deist, which many of America's founding fathers claimed to be, believed in a God who created the universe and then walked away. Therefore a God could exist, even be worshiped, and at the same time human reason would become the final authority.

Some have conjectured that while the roots of modernity were evident many years before, the actual birth of modernism was in 1789 at the fall of the Bastille in France during the French Revolution. Gene Edward Veith reasons, 'The French Revolution exemplifies the triumph of the Enlightenment. With the destruction of the Bastille, the prison in which the monarchy jailed its political prisoners, the pre-modern world with its feudal loyalties and spiritual hierarchies was guillotined. The revolutionaries exalted the Rights of Man. They dismissed Christianity as a relic of the past. During the course of the revolution, they installed the Goddess of Reason in Notre Dame Cathedral.'[3]

As with all worldviews, except the biblical one, modernity would ultimately disappoint. People became disenchanted with reason and science, as neither was able to deliver on their promises to solve all human problems and reshape society into utopia. So disappointed did the Western world became with modernism that it finally breathed its last and has been pronounced dead. The date of modernity's death has been a matter of much speculation. Some believe it was at the fall of the Berlin Wall in 1989 (exactly 200 years after its birth) since, of all social experiments, Marxism most fully attempted to implement the concepts of the Enlightenment. When Communism crumbled so did the last vestiges of the optimism in human ability that for so long propelled modernity. Others believe that, at least in America, modernity died on 15 July 1973, with the demolition of the Pruitt-Igoe housing projects in St. Louis. It was at that moment that Americans threw in the towel on their own utopian experiments, recognizing that reason, science, and technology had failed to enhance the lives of the poor and had actually brought more misery.

Whether modernity died in 1973 or 1989 may be debatable, but that it is dead is not. That is not to deny that many aspects of our society still operate under the vestiges of modernistic principles (and premodern for that matter), but an obvious shift has taken place in the mindset and worldview of the Western civilization. The new worldview is called postmodernism.

Postmodernism

Postmodernism was born out of the ashes of the failure of modernity. It is the reaction of the disillusioned. If the optimistic projections of the last two hundred years of the best efforts of reason, science and technology have failed; and if the tenets of premodernism with its foundation of revelatory truth are preposterous, then all that is left is the pessimism of nothingness, emptiness and uncertainty. Perhaps never has the book of Ecclesiastes been more relevant than now.

Postmodernity is relatively complicated, so it is necessary to probe carefully its worldview and its effect on cultures as well as the church. At this point we simply want to recognize that at the hub of this philosophy, as well as all philosophies, is the issue of truth. To the premodernist, truth is found in revelation. To the modernist, truth can be found in reason and science. To the postmodernist truth is not found (indeed it is not capable of being found), it is created. Absolute truth is a fable. It is possible for me to create my own truth, and for cultures and subcultures to create their truth, but it is not possible to find universal truth that is applicable to all people. Such truth does not exist and should not be sought. Those who claim to possess absolute truth only do so in order to assert power over others.

Kruger explains,

> Postmodernity, in contrast to modernity, rejects any notion of objective truth and insists that the only absolute in the universe is that there are no absolutes. Tolerance is the supreme virtue and exclusivity the supreme vice. Truth is not grounded in reality or in any sort of authoritative "text", but is simply constructed by the mind of the individual [or socially constructed].[4]

Groothuis elaborates, 'For these postmodernist thinkers, the very idea of truth has decayed and disintegrated. It is no longer something knowable... At the end of the day, truth is simply what we, as individuals and as communities, make it to be — and nothing more.'[5] If this is so, then how do people make decisions and develop values, or even create their own truth? Kruger answers, 'What are the postmodernists' criteria for "truth"? Simply what works. The postmodernist is not concerned about absolute truth like the modernist; he defines his "truth" by more pragmatic concerns: What makes me feel good? What solves my problems? What is attractive to me?'[6] This concept of truth will be important to keep in mind as we study this worldview in more detail.

The reader may properly wonder, is not all of this postmodern philosophy a mere intellectual football being tossed about by the elite? Has this mentality really trickled down to masses? Unfortunately, surveys confirm that while the majority may be unable to define postmodernity they are increasingly becoming products of it. For a number of years Barna Research Group has been telling us that belief in absolute truth hovered at around 38% in America. That means that almost two out of every three adults in America deny the existence of absolute truth. But things have gotten worse. At the end of 2001, just a few months after the infamous 9/11 attacks, an alarming survey was conducted by Barna that found confidence in absolute moral truth had dropped to a mere 22%.[7] Barely one in five Americans claim to believe in absolute truth, which is amazing considering, that according to Barna's research, one out of every three Americans claim to be an *evangelical* Christian. And America seems to fare better than many other countries. Take Europe for example. While 53% of Americans consider religion to be very important in their lives, only 16% of the British, 14% of the French and 13% of Germans do.[8] In addition, the citizens of the United Kingdom are less likely to believe in God than those in most countries. A survey conducted by the BBC in January of 2004 discovered that 67% believed in a Higher Being (vs. 91% of those in the U.S.), but only 31% (compared to 51% in the U.S.) agreed that their God was the only true God.[9]

In other words, we not only live in a postmodern era (we can't help that) but most of us have become postmodernist — even many who claim to be Christians. If this is not recognized and confronted we will inevitably interact with a world and church that we presume to be modernistic in thinking when they are not. We then run the danger of driving in one ditch or the other. In the first ditch are those who accommodate the spirit of the age. The liberals did this in the nineteenth and twentieth centuries by accepting modernism and denying the supernatural, including the cardinal doctrines of the faith. Unfortunately, those within the Christian community who have been on the cutting edge of watching the shift to postmodernism are wandering down the same pathway taken by the liberals of one hundred years ago. The market-driven, or seeker-sensitive, church leaders understand that the 'consumer' now thinks like postmoderns. These leaders have decided that the only way to win postmoderns is to give them what they think they need in hope of giving them what they really need. This approach of accommodation has been tried before with disastrous and predictable results. In the other ditch run those who refuse to recognize that the world has changed. They run the risk of obsolescence. But there is an approach, a biblical one, in which we can remain faithful to the Word and yet speak to our age.

2

Whatever Happened to Truth?

The main character in Jean-Paul Sartre's famous novel *Nausea*, examines life carefully and comes to these gloomy conclusions:

> I was just thinking, that here we sit, all of us, eating and drinking to preserve our precious existence and really there is nothing, nothing, absolutely no reason for existing... I exist — the world exists — and I know that the world exists. That's all. It makes no difference to me... Every existing thing is born without reason, prolongs itself out of weakness and dies by chance... I do not believe in God; His existence is belied by science. But, in the internment camp, I learned to believe in men.[1]

Sartre was a leading proponent of the philosophical system known as existentialism, which was a reaction to the materialistic optimism of modernity with its infinite faith in reason and science. The existentialist measured life by other criteria and decided that it really was meaningless and absurd. Truth and purpose could not be found in science or reason, for that matter, it could not even be found in revelation. Truth, if truth exists at all, could only be found within the individual. Truth, then, is a personal matter. It is not something one searches for and finds; it is something one creates for himself. Your truth may not be truth for me and I may therefore reject it, for truth is not universal, it is individualistic. But this fact does not negate that truth for you. You can embrace your truth and I can embrace mine, but we dare not attempt to impose our truth on anyone else. To claim to have found truth is a deceitful tool by which we attempt to manipulate and control one another. It is a power play, pure and simple.

It is from this fountain of existential philosophical thought that postmodernism has sprung. Postmodernity has adjusted and expanded the teachings of existentialism, but its connection is unquestionable, as we will see as we outline some of the basic tenets of the system. The reader might be warned that much within postmodernism is complicated, ridiculous and contradictory. It is a system that makes little sense and is basically unworkable. Nevertheless it is the mood of the moment and has infiltrated the thinking of countless people in our society.

Rejection of universal truth

That the rejection of truth lies at the centre of postmodernity must be grasped to have any kind of handle on what is being taught. As with existentialism, there is a rejection of absolute truth. As in existentialism, truth is not found. It is created. But unlike existentialism, truth is constructed not individually but socially. That is, individual societies, cultures and subcultures develop *their truth* to which members of that community must adhere. However, this socially constructed truth is subject to change and is highly subjective.

When Pilate asked Jesus, 'What is truth?' he surely was not calling for a debate, but every philosophical and religious system before and since has dealt with that question. The prevalent answers to the truth question in Western society today are rooted in one of three sources: Scripture, the Enlightenment, or postmodernism. 'In the biblical view, truth is that which is ultimately, finally, and absolutely real, or the "way it is", and therefore is utterly trustworthy and dependable, being grounded in God's own reality and truthfulness'[2] — and I would add, is revealed in Scripture. The Enlightenment placed faith in rationalism, which taught that truth is knowable by the unaided intellect of the sincere truth seeker.

Revelation was not needed; reason and science could provide the answers. It was under the influence of Enlightenment thinking that the framers of America's Declaration of Independence would state, 'We hold these truths to be self-evident.' Truth, not revealed by God but self-evident to the reasoning mind, was the hallmark of the Enlightenment.[3] Some have claimed in recent times that fundamental/evangelical thinking is nothing but a product of the Enlightenment. Mark Noll (professor at Wheaton College), for example, has stated, 'Virtually *every* aspect of the profound evangelical attachment to the Bible was shaped by the Enlightenment.'[4] But the rationalism of the Enlightenment, as Iain Murray tells us 'is a use of the mind, which trusts in its own ability to arrive at truth about God without his aid and apart from revelation: it treats the mind as a source of knowledge rather than as a channel'.[5] So the Enlightenment and modernity teach the ultimate source of authority in the pursuit of truth is human reason; the Bible claims that source is found in the revelation of Scripture — a huge difference that Professor Noll has ignored.

So what does postmodernity propose? Kruger answers, 'What are the postmodernists' criteria for "truth"? Simply what works. Postmodernists are not concerned about absolute truth like the modernist; they define their 'truth' by more pragmatic concerns: What makes me feel good? What solves my problems? What is attractive to me?'[6] Os Guinness is therefore right when he observes that due to postmodernism's assault on truth and reason 'objective, experimental, scientific data [has been replaced] with personal, anecdotal experience [as the source of truth in society]'.[7] In the Christian world things are not a lot better.

Of course, if truth, at the end of the day, is unknowable in any objective sense, and is reduced to what is good for 'me', where does that lead us? To chaos, confusion and the 'grand sez who'. Groothuis writes, 'If God is not invoked as the ultimate evaluator, the One whose words constitute moral truth… why should a given legal system be endorsed? Why should selves legislate morality…? Why should we seek the greatest happiness for the greatest number? What makes the Constitution the proper glue for our society? Says who?'[8] He then quotes this rather sacrilegious poem,

Napalming babies is bad
Starving the poor is wicked.
Buying and selling each other is wicked.
Those who stood up to and died resisting Hitler, Stalin, Amin,
   and Pol
Pot — and General Custer too — have earned salvation.
Those who acquiesced deserved to be damned.
There is in the world such a thing as evil.
(All together now:) Sez who?
God help us.[9]

Relativism

Postmodern societies seem workable as long as communities, with their individualized brand of truth, stay isolated. But what happens when societies, each packing their own understanding of truth, collide? How is a country like America, with its melting pot of religions, ethnic backgrounds and the like, going to exist? By adopting a relativism mindset, which recognizes everyone's truth as equal. Since there is no absolute truth anyway, your view is as good as mine. We should all live and let live; and by no means ever impose our understanding of right, wrongs, morals, and ethics on those of another philosophical community. This is the ultimate sin, perhaps the only sin, in a postmodern world.

To a postmodernist an individual culture really does not traffic in truth, it tells stories — something they like to call narratives. To these thinkers, claims of truth are fictional, hence stories. When people develop a worldview all they are doing is telling a story (fiction) about stories (fiction), which is called a metanarrative. When all the dust has settled and the fancy words and ideas are reduced to their essence, what we have is a worldview that denies worldviews. In other words a true universal worldview is impossible because absolute truth is impossible. We may have values, morals, and concepts that work for us, or our subculture, but we cannot expect other subcultures to adopt our understandings for they may not work for them. Truth is simply that which works for a particular community and nothing more.

A particularly interesting (and destructive) aspect of this is that postmodernists feel perfectly free to rewrite history to suit their own agenda. This freedom is warranted, they believe, because historical accounts are little more than fiction anyway, created by those who were attempting to manipulate and control the masses. Since history is a power play why not arrange it so as to accommodate our own interests now? A couple of examples of this would be helpful. Take first the historical/dramas of the modern media. Whether the facts support the murder of John Kennedy, the assassination of the Pope or the improper/immoral relationship of Thomas Jefferson with his slaves, does not matter. We are free to present history as we like, as long as we place the disclaimer that "some" of the events are fictional. Another good example would be the recent amnesia on the part of Westerners concerning the past Islamic/ Christian conflicts in general and the Crusades in particular. Until recently both the Christian and Islamic communities were in agreement that the Crusades were part of a mutual contest between the two religions, a conflict that Muslims initiated. But such sentiments are nowhere to be found today.[10] It is fashionable to believe wicked Christians attempted to annihilate the innocent and peace loving Muslims, which is a complete distortion and rewriting of history. In any other age such fabrications would be revealed and debunked, but in this postmodern era they are embraced.

Deconstructionism

Nothing is more important in the comprehension of postmodernism than its convoluted, incredible view of language. Veith says it well,

> Postmodernists base this new relativism and the view that all meaning is socially constructed on a particular view of language. This set of theories, along with the analytical method that they make possible, can be referred to as "deconstruction."... Postmodernist theories begin with the assumption that language cannot render truths about the world in an objective way. Language, by its very nature,

shapes what we think, Since language is a cultural creation, meaning is ultimately (again) a social construction.[11]

Kruger adds, 'Deconstructionism has relegated all texts to simply societal constructions — i.e., the reader's own experience and
perspective so conditions interpretations that there can be no one
"right" interpretation.'[12]

A couple of observations are immediately apparent with reference to deconstructionism. First, if words have no objective meaning; and all interpretation lies in the mind of the reader (hearer),
then the logical deduction is that communication is impossible. Ad-
ditionally, the reasoning, logic, and pronouncements of the postmodernist proponents are just as preposterous as anyone else's. If
the content of their words have no meaning, apart from the meaning you or I choose to give them, then they have nothing meaningful to say. Of course, that does not stop them from saying it.

Secondly, the evidence of deconstruction within Christian circles is striking. It is becoming increasingly rare for Bible studies,
sermons and Christian books to be based on proper hermeneutical
methods. Rather, 'what does it mean to me' is in vogue. Iain Murray, in his excellent book, *Evangelicalism Divided*, quotes Michael
Saward as he surveys the evangelical scene of the 1980s that laid
the groundwork for the postmodern church,

> This is the disturbing legacy of the 1960s and 1970s. A gen-
> eration brought up on guitars, choruses, and home group
> discussion. Educated, as one of them put it to me, not to
> use words with precision because the image is dominant,
> not the word. Equipped not to handle doctrine but rather to
> "share". A compassionate, caring generation, suspicious of
> definition and labels, uneasy at, and sometimes incapable
> of, being asked to wrestle with sustained didactic exposi-
> tion of theology. Excellent when it comes to providing reli-
> gious music, drama, and art. Not so good when asked to
> preach and teach the Faith.[13]

How the postmodern worldview has infected society and the
church will be the subject of our next two chapters.

3

'Postmodernity and Society'

Having raced far too briefly through an overview of postmodernism,[1] we will now turn our attention to an equally brief account of this worldview's impact on society. Let's begin with Western culture. Since absolute truth has been rejected, how does a postmodern society function? There exists a number of identifiable pillars propping up the postmodern vision — each of these pillars depend upon the others to prevent collapse of the system. As we will see, postmodernity is an inconsistent philosophy at best.

Truth is communal

We documented in an earlier chapter that while postmodernity rejects absolute, universal truth, it does not reject all standards of truth. Drawing from the well of existentialism, which championed individualized truth, this newer worldview (which by the way claims to reject worldviews) believes in communal truth. That is, each culture creates its own truth, and the citizens of that culture are expected to adhere to their community's concept of truth with its attached morals and values.

Of course, it does not take a genius to recognize that such a view is fraught with irresolvable problems. First, if multitudes of communities each have their own version of truth and those versions are at odds on many issues, then 'true truth', as Francis Schaeffer used to say, cannot exist. Postmodernists recognize this little problem which is why they claim there is no true truth, only stories (or narratives). All pronouncements of truth are ultimately fiction. There is no final truth. If this is the case, the next problem to be faced is the dialogue between communities. As Groothuis states, 'With these assumptions locked in place, any meaningful communication between, say, Aborigines and white Australians or white Americans and Native Americans would be impossible in principle. Each culture creates truth through its language, and language cannot refer to extralinguistic realities.'[2]

This leads to a third problem. What happens when cultures, with their own fictional version of truth, clash? Americans call terrorism murder, but Islamic fundamentalists call it justifiable casualties during time of war. Who is right? Under postmodernism right or wrong can't be determined because each culture operates under a different system of truth. A consistent American postmodern disciple might mourn the events surrounding 9/11 (based upon the Western society's value on life) but they could not denounce the actions, which are rooted in the Islamic fundamentalist subculture's value system. Living with a postmodern worldview is complicated, and when all the rhetoric is over, ultimately impossible.

Pluralism

It must first be admitted (and postmodern thinkers do so) that Western culture is still deeply dependent upon the borrowed capital of Christianity, along with its moral fiber and handle on truth and values. For example, a consistent postmodernist would have to agree that if a subculture found it morally acceptable to murder babies, gas Jews or enslave Blacks, then no one has the right to object. But of course postmodernists can't live with such consequences of their own philosophy. They are grateful, for the time being, that they have a backup system such as Christianity, or else total anarchy would reign.

Still, the postmodernists cling gamely to the ideal of pluralism. We are told regularly by the media that we live in a pluralistic society, thus we must live and let live. At all cost, we must not even insinuate that we have the truth, for not only are such pronouncements offensive to others, they are downright arrogant. Carson writes, 'Philosophical pluralism has generated many approaches in support of one stance: namely, that any notion that a particular ideological or religious claim is intrinsically superior to another is *necessarily* wrong. The only absolute creed is the creed of pluralism. No religion has the right to pronounce itself right or true, and the others false, or even (in the majority view) relatively inferior (emphasis in the original).'[3]

Once again this reduces all of life to the telling of fictional stories. How can people with such an understanding of life make decisions and navigate without extreme frustration? They can do so only because they have accepted the idea of contradictory thinking.

By the way, a new understanding of tolerance is in vogue under postmodernity. Tolerance of people, even while rejecting their ideas was one of the linchpins of early democracy. Tolerance now means we must accept everyone's ideas as equally valid. To be critical of anyone's ideas is a sign of intolerance — which cannot be tolerated (the irony is obvious).

Contradictory thinking

D. A. Carson gives the following example of the first generation raised in a postmodern age: 'It is said that baby busters do not want to be lectured; they expect to be entertained. They prefer videos to books; many of them have not learned to think in a linear fashion; they put more store than they recognize in mere impressions. As a result, they can live with all sorts of logical inconsistencies and be totally unaware of them. How many times have I tried to explain to a university-age young person who has made some profession of faith that it is fundamentally inconsistent to claim to know and love the God of the Bible, while cohabiting with someone?'[4]

The ability to believe contradictory things simultaneously is a hallmark of postmodern thinking. A few years ago Barna Research Group documented that two thirds of Americans do not believe in absolute truth (this number has recently risen to 78%).[5] To claim to believe absolute truth does not exist is a self-contradiction in itself, for that claim must be based on a belief in something that is true — in this case that truth does not exist (gets complicated doesn't it?). So the one absolute allowed in postmodern thought is that absolutes do not exist. But it gets worse, for the same Barna poll showed that 53 percent of evangelical Christians believe there are no absolutes.[6] Veith makes this comment about these statistics,

> This means the majority of those who say that they believe in the authority of the Bible and know Christ as their Savior nevertheless agree that 'there is no such thing as absolute truth'. Not Christ? No, although He presumably 'works for them'. Not the Bible? Apparently not, although 88 percent of evangelicals believe that 'The Bible is the written Word of God and is totally accurate in all it teaches.' Bizarrely, 70 percent of all Americans claim to accept this high view of Scripture, which is practically the same number of those who say 'there are no absolutes'.[7]

This kind of contradictory thinking would be unacceptable in any other age but is common place today, even among Christians. Only in such an intellectual environment could the very same people embrace scores of competing ideologies. Take the field of psychology, which is almost universally trusted in the West. 'If you need psychiatric help, you might be treated by a Freudian, a Jungian, a humanist, or a behaviorist. Your treatment might consist of telling about your childhood, recording your dreams, getting in touch with your feeling, or exposing yourself to operant conditioning. The philosophies behind these psychological theories are incompatible — Freud and the behaviorists cannot both be right — and the methodologies are untestable.'[8] But little contradictions like these do not matter in a postmodern era. It does not matter if competing therapies are mutually exclusive, all can be believed, although rational thinking would tell us that this is impossible.

Finally, what about ethics? 'A Zogby International Poll of college seniors came up with a fascinating finding. Almost all of the 401 randomly selected students around the country — 97 percent — said their college studies had prepared them to behave ethically in their future work lives. So far so good. But 73 percent of the students said that when their professors taught about ethical issues, the usual message was that uniform standards of right and wrong don't exist ("what is right and wrong depends on differences in individual values and cultural diversity")... Since "truth" is an act of community empowerment, truth is whatever the tribe or the individual says it is.'[9] So we are left with each individual or community choosing his or her own ethical and moral standards. If those standards contradict, then so be it. This is the only generation in history which has been able to declare contradictory and mutually exclusive claims on truth, ethics, morals, and values to be equally valid.

Power Plays

Since the one absolute accepted by postmodernist is that there exists absolutely no absolutes, how do postmodernists view those who claim to possess some form of absolute truth? With suspicion. Whether in the realm of history, religion, science or even medicine, the postmodern thinker believes that all truth claims are attempts to manipulate others. In other words, truth claims are nothing more that cover-ups for power plays. The only reason anyone would claim to know anything with certainty, since such a thing is impossible, is because they want to empower themselves and enslave others. One author gives these examples, 'If the Declaration of Independence declares "all men to be created equal", it thus excludes women and since Thomas Jefferson owned slaves, it is no doubt a white, European male power play over the rest of society. Since the Bible uses the masculine pronoun in referring to God the Father, the Bible is merely a history of a male-dominated religion that must be rejected if we care anything about women.'[10]

Postmodernist thinkers have covered themselves well. They have denied absolute truth and any who would challenge them are intolerant power hungry tyrants seeking to impose their wishes on others.

4

'Postmodernity and the Church'

At certain points in history the church has served as a rebuke to the secular mindset of society. At such times Christians have challenged and exposed the popular fads that ruled the day, revealing those fads for what they were, shallow and empty, mere 'broken cisterns that can hold no water' (Jer. 2:13). Sadly, now is not one of those points in history. Rather, the Christian community at the present time appears to be in lock step with the world system. Whatever the world is selling Christians seem to be buying. They may perfume it a bit, hang some religious ornaments on it, and throw some scriptures into the mix, but when stripped to its essence evangelicals frequently find themselves mimicking the world's philosophy.

We find this true with regard to postmodernity. Rather than repel the forces leading this ungodly worldview, we have welcomed them into our camp, adapted their most appetizing features and structured our ministries according to their market research. What polls and surveys have to say seem to carry considerably more weight in today's local church than what the apostle Paul had to say.

Culture has always influenced the church, but in a real sense the postmodern culture has engulfed the church — and in many cases defined the church. We see its fingerprints everywhere we turn. We want to investigate some of the most obvious evidence of postmodernity's influence within the evangelical community in this chapter. It will not be a pretty sight. Then in our final chapter on this subject we will address some of the means by which we can withstand the onslaught of this philosophical system.

In what ways has the postmodern worldview, which has only been in full bloom for less than two decades, impacted the evangelical community? Consider the following:

A felt needs gospel

Gene Veith tells the story of an evangelical church which wanted to grow numerically and decided to use postmodern strategy. First came the market survey, which pinpointed a number of steps necessary to implement such growth in a postmodern age. For example, it was determined that the church must change its name because the term 'Baptist' was a turn off in the community. And people would only come to church if it were convenient, so it was necessary to relocate to a prime location off the freeway. A modern facility was erected with all the bells and whistles that reflect a materialistic society. On the other hand religious symbols, such as the cross, were offensive to some, so the symbols were expunged. Not only symbols but words are offensive as well; it became necessary, therefore, to eliminate terms such as redemption and conversion. Of course, negative subjects such as hell and judgment had to be replaced with positive ones. 'In abandoning its doctrine and its moral authority and in adjusting its teaching to the demands of the market place, the church embarked on a pilgrimage to postmodernism.'[1]

What is happening? Having discovered postmodernists' disdain for truth, the postmodern church has determined that the lost will never be reached through the offer of authoritative truth. To claim to be in possession of absolutes is viewed suspiciously today, since it is a thinly disguised power grab, so we are better off not playing the 'truth' card too openly. In order to reach the citizens of this age we must give them what they want. And what do they want? They want to have their felt-needs met and they want to have a religious experience. If we desire to attract people to Christ these days, we are told, we need to understand their mindset. The old gospel of redemption from sin, righteousness in Christ and a future in heaven with our Lord just doesn't play well any more.

I have documented this mentality toward evangelism from primary sources in my book *This Little Church Went to Market*, so I will not repeat those things here. But read some of the observations by respected Christian leaders who see what has happened. D. A. Carson writes,

> Weigh how many presentations of the gospel have been 'eased' by portraying Jesus as the One who fixes marriages, ensures the American dream, cancels loneliness, gives us power, and generally makes us happy. He is portrayed that way primarily because in our efforts to make Jesus appear relevant we *have cast the human dilemma in merely contemporary categories, taking our cues from the perceived needs of the day.* But if we follow Scripture, and understand that the fundamental needs of the race are irrefragably tied to the Fall, we will follow the Bible as it sets out God's gracious solution to that fundamental need; *and then the gospel we preach will be less skewed by the contemporary agenda...* If you begin with perceived needs, you will always distort the gospel. If you begin with the Bible's definition of our need, relating perceived needs to that central grim reality, you are more likely to retain intact the gospel of God (emphasis in the original).[2]

Douglas Groothuis laments, 'Some Christians are hailing postmodernism as the trend that will make the church interesting and exciting to postmoderns. We are told that Christians must shift their emphasis from objective truth to communal experience, from rational argument to subjective appeal, from doctrinal orthodoxy to "relevant" practices. I have reasoned throughout this book that this move is nothing less than fatal to Christian integrity and biblical witness. It is also illogical philosophically. We have something far better to offer.'[3]

Veith is on the mark when he comments,

Instead of preaching that leads to the conviction of sin and salvation through the cross of Jesus Christ, the churches preach 'feel-good' messages designed to cheer people up. Some have described postmodernist culture as a 'therapeutic culture', in which a sense of psychological well-being, not truth, is the controlling value. The contemporary church likewise faces the temptation to replace theology with therapy... Evangelism, according to this model, does not involve proclaiming God's judgment against sinners and His gracious offer of salvation through faith in Jesus Christ. Rather, evangelism simply educates people as to how much God loves them. God really does not want to punish anyone; He wants all to feel good about themselves, to lead a full life, to be happy. Those who turn away from God will miss out on this abundant life, though the Holy Spirit may well bring them to Heaven even though they never knew Christ.[4]

It is no wonder then that Groothuis shares one of my concerns: 'One great danger of postmodernity is false conversions and the consequently hollow praise offered to God for saved souls that, in fact, are not saved. Those holding to a postmodernist view of truth may appear very "spiritual", and to go along with Christian belief to a point, just so long as religion meets their felt needs. Nevertheless, unless one knows Jesus Christ and his gospel to be true, one cannot be a Christian at all. One remains entrapped in the kingdom of darkness.'[5]

All the other ways that postmodernity impacts the church today are tied closely with this issue of the felt-need gospel.

Inclusivism

Following closely on the heels of the new age gospel message is the necessary rise in the popularity of inclusivism, or the idea that the Lord has sheep in other religions — some who will never hear the name of Christ. Inclusivism teaches that adult adherents of other religions can be saved by being good followers of their own religions. This is the natural conclusion of pluralism. If no one is right, then everyone is right. Who are evangelical Christians to make the absurd claim that only they have found the key to eternal life? Such an attitude we expect from the unbeliever but as postmodernism invades the church, inclusivism is rapidly being accepted there as well. Even Billy Graham seems to have embraced inclusivism. He stated in a television interview with Robert Schuller, 'Whether they come from the Muslim world, or the Buddhist world or the non-believing world, they are members of the Body of Christ because they have been called by God. They may not know the name of Jesus but they know in their hearts that they need something they do not have, and they turn to the only light they have and I think that they are saved and they are going to be with us in heaven.'[6]

A mystical/pragmatic faith

If truth is nonexistent, as the postmodernist insists, then by default we are left with religious experiences devoid of objective content and pragmatism. Biblical Christianity has always run counter to both these errors. Colossians chapter two, for example, warns of trading in the substance found in the true knowledge of Christ for the shadows of mysticism and empty philosophies of a godless age. We dare not allow our times to mould our theology. Os Guinness warns,

> Whereas both the Bible and the best thinkers of Christian history invite seekers to put their faith in God because the message conveying that invitation is true, countless Christians today believe for various other reasons. For instance, they believe faith is true, 'because it works' (pragmatism), because they 'feel it is true in their experience' (subjectivism), because they sincerely believe it is 'true for them' (relativism), and so on… The Christian faith is not true because it works; it works because it is true. It is not true because we experience it; we experience it — deeply and gloriously — because it is true.[7]

Postmodern Christians have reversed this order and now evaluate all truth claims and doctrine by experience. The notion that we know certain things to be true (at least true for us) because we have had some experience is running rampant within Christendom. And woe to the one who would insinuate that someone's experience does not meet the test of Scripture. Such a person is judgmental and critical, and worst of all negative. So when experience and mysticism become the litmus test for truth in our personal life, we would expect that it would shape our corporate worship as well — and it has.

Worship services

If experience is the chief goal of our personal spiritual lives, then we should expect that experience would become the chief goal of our public worship as well. Too often the music, the prayers, and even the sermons are attempts to arouse emotions and provide an experience rather than convey truth. Monte Wilson is correct when he writes,

> For the modern evangelical, worship is defined *exclusively* in terms of the individual experience. Worship, then, is not about adoring God but about being nourished with religious feelings, so much so that the worshiper has become the object of worship. When we study the ancient approach to worship, however, we see that the church did not overly concern itself with feelings of devotion, but rather with heartfelt and biblically informed obedience... Others probably the majority in modern American evangelicalism — having utterly neglected any commitment to the content of the Word and have ended with narcissistic 'worship' services where everyone drowns in a sea of subjectivism and calls it 'being bathed in the presence of the Holy Spirit'. These people come to church exclusively to 'feel' God (emphasis in the original).[8]

Postmodernity has even changed the preaching. In an article advocating leaving expository preaching for story-telling, George

Barna says, 'Busters are non-linear, comfortable with contradictions, and inclined to view all religions as equally valid. The nice
thing about telling stories is that no one can say your story isn't
true.'[9] And so, Christian postmodernists advocate leaving the authority of the Word of God because Busters will not believe it, and
replacing it with the authority of 'my story'. We have to wonder, as
the modern unbeliever takes a look at the modern church, are they
seeing anything but their own reflection?

5

'Confronting Postmodernists'

In previous chapters I have discussed postmodernity's encroachment on Western society and on the church, and identified the dangers and impact of this worldview. What do we do now? I believe we must be willing to go against the grain of a condoning society and display some holy intolerance. Doing so will surely be painful. We will be disliked, misunderstood, even vilified — but of course we will be in good company. Jesus, the prophets and the apostles all suffered a similar fate at the hands of unbelievers and sometimes even fellow believers. But did not Jesus pronounce us blessed when 'men cast insults at you, and persecute you, and say all kinds of evil against you falsely, on account of Me' (Matt. 5:11)? This is not the time to cave into the pressures that surround us; it is the time to take our stand for the truth. Pascal wrote:

> And is it not obvious that, just as it is a crime to disturb the peace when truth reigns, it is also a crime to remain at peace when the truth is being destroyed? There is therefore a time when peace is just and a time when it is unjust. Weaklings are those who know the truth, but maintain it only as far as it is in their interest to do so, and apart from that forsake it.[1]

While there are a number of fronts on which we must fight the postmodern worldview, we will catalogue and comment on four.

The truth front

It is along the truth front that the hottest battles have always been waged by God's people. What is different today is that now the very existence of truth is under attack. The postmodernist questions the reality of truth and is suspicious of any who claim possession of it. Thus, the issue of truth is not an important one for this generation; they are far more interested in how they feel, their experiences (spiritual or otherwise) and having their needs met. This being the case, we are not surprised to find that 'some church-growth advocates advise that churches tone down any emphasis on the objective truth of Christian doctrine because postmoderns have short attention spans and are only interested in their own felt needs... [A George Barna survey reinforced this approach, stating that over half of evangelicals agreed with this statement]: "The purpose of life is enjoyment and personal fulfillment."'[2]

I believe this recent advice by the seeker-sensitive church to be the very worst route that we could possibly take. First, historically, this methodology has precedents of disastrous proportions. One of the most obvious examples is the founding of liberalism. The father of modern liberalism (which ultimately denied almost all scriptural truth) is considered to be Friedrich Schleiermacher (1768-1834). Schleiermacher's basic philosophy seemed benign enough, and not that far from conservative theology. He believed religion is primarily not a matter of doctrine, but of feeling, intuition and experience. But once that door was opened the fundamentals of the faith quickly began to evaporate. Soon Schleiermacher was instructing his students that the creation of an experience, not the teaching of the Word, was to be the object of the preacher. Liberalism, in the early years, rarely challenged cardinal doctrines directly. On the contrary, it claimed the authority of the New Testament for the view that Christianity is life, not doctrine (a battle cry we often hear today in evangelical circles). The fallout of liberal theology is evident in the twenty-first century, yet strangely its basic tenets are being mimicked today by the church growth experts (apparently without knowledge that they are doing so).

What should be our response? Do we simply 'adjust' the teachings of Scripture to accommodate the whims of a deceived people?

Certainly not — we must challenge the darkened understanding of our age, as did all the prophets and apostles (not to mention our Lord) in their age. Generally speaking our approach must be two-pronged. First, we must boldly proclaim truth. The godly found in Scripture never soft-peddled or minimized the message to avoid offending the sensitivities of the masses. Paul's approach was not to debate or manipulate, but to preach the wisdom of God (1 Cor. 2). His message was foolishness to the philosophically trained Greeks and a stumbling block to the Jews, but that did not discourage him, for he knew that to the called it was the power of God (1 Cor. 1:23, 24). The proclamation of truth is politically incorrect at the moment, and despised by the majority, but nevertheless, it is the only prescription that God has given for life and godliness. We will never heal broken souls by offering them a watered-down solution.

There is a second prong to our stance. Even as we proclaim truth we must recognize that postmodern individuals filter what we say through their own worldview. Michael Kruger is correct when he writes, 'If a Christian engages a non-Christian in a debate without challenging his overarching worldview, then his effectiveness will be minimal; each side is playing by its own set of rules ... [Therefore the Christian must challenge] their opponents' criteria for truth by showing that it should be God's Word.'[3] In discussing how to do this, let's move to the next front under attack, the Scriptures.

The Scripture front

It is virtually impossible to separate truth from the Word of God. A belief in the authority of the Bible would spell the death of post-modernity. The problem is not only do we live in a postmodern era, but we also live in a post-Christian era that is accompanied by an abysmal lack of scriptural knowledge. Many university students don't know that the Bible has two testaments. They have no knowledge of even the main characters in the Scriptures, and certainly no understanding of the biblical message or worldview.

The evangelical church must shoulder much of the blame for the drainage of scriptural knowledge from our society, a knowledge that was commonplace only a few decades ago. Far too concerned with excellence in our musical productions, entertainment of our young people, and creation of worshipful experiences, we have all but neglected the systematic teaching of the Word. Surely our churches are still bulging with Bible studies, lectures and even sermons, but it is becoming increasingly rare to find the Word of God maintaining its centrality in the Christian community. Bible studies are often a mere sharing of ignorance, sermons are seldom expository and pastors and conference speakers work hard at keeping their audience happy and meeting their felt needs. Ministers are being trained, not to be shepherds of the flock, but presidents of a corporation. As a result, not only is the unbeliever ignorant of the Word, but often the Christian also is as well. Ignorant Christians live foolish lives as they bounce from mystical experience to entertaining programming in hopes of finding an anchor. A return to the priority of the Word is the great need of the moment.

But there is a problem. Fuelling this slide from scriptural understanding is a fundamental change in the hermeneutics with which we approach Scripture. The postmodern worldview has infiltrated how we interpret Scripture. Terms such as 'new hermeneutics', 'radical hermeneutics' and 'deconstruction', while unfamiliar to the average Christian, nevertheless define a 'new approach' to Bible study that stems straight from the postmodern textbooks. When we hear someone deny the obvious understanding of a passage of Scripture with, 'Well, that is your interpretation', we are in the presence of a postmodern Christian, whether they have ever heard the term or not. This approach infuses all the meaning of a given passage in the reader, not in the text. Interpretation is subjective, not objective. When we come to a text of Scripture, we are told, we bring with us our biases and backgrounds so that the true meaning of the text is hopelessly lost to us. All that matters is what we think the text says — what it means to us. And 'because meaning finally resides in the interpreter, there are as many meanings as there are interpreters... That means no one meaning can ever be thought to be superior to any other meaning; there is no objective basis on which to evaluate them.'[4]

So there we have it. We can now, thanks to postmodern hermeneutics, make great claim to being the followers of the Word of God, while undermining its very authority — at the same time having no concept of what has happened. The solution is as simple as it is profound. We must return to the absolute authority of Scripture, to normal (i.e. grammatical-historical) hermeneutics, and to the centrality of the Word in our lives and churches. We must let the Bible speak for itself. It matters little what 'it means to me'. What matters is what it means to God. Our job is to discern God's meaning and apply it to our lives.

The evangelistic/apologetic front

A mistake often made by Christians is the attempt to out-debate the unbeliever through the use of evidence. If we could prove creation scientifically, if we could show beyond doubt the historical accuracy of Jesus, if Noah's ark could be found, etc., then the non-Christian would lay down his arms and join our ranks. This is naïve at best. While there is certainly a place for showing the rationale of our faith, the fact of the matter is that the unsaved reject the gospel because their 'foolish heart is darkened' (Rom. 1:21). The message of Romans 1:18-32 is that God has planted knowledge of himself within the heart of all mankind (v. 19) and has demonstrated his existence through his creation (v. 20), but the lost have chosen to suppress that truth in unrighteousness (v. 18). They would rather live out their sinfulness than bow before their Lord.

In the age of postmodernity the presupposition of the lost is that absolute truth is not a relevant issue. Until this is addressed we are often not even speaking the same language. For this reason, I believe that while we proclaim truth we must also undermine the listener's worldview. Perhaps the best way to do this is to show that the postmodern philosophical system is unworkable — it is unliveable. For instance, postmodern advocates might say that everything is relative, but if someone throws a rock through their windshield or steals their money, they will complain loudly and clearly. They may declare slavery, or the Holocaust, or terrorist bombings as evil, but they have no logical base for their declaration. The Holocaust may be immoral in their community but not in the Nazi community of the 1940s. Their system simply cannot work, for it cannot stand on its own merits. Ultimately, postmoderns are able to function because they steal liberally from the benefits of the Christian worldview. Their worldview provides no foundation to pronounce anything as wrong — or right. It is because of these obvious weaknesses that the leaders in postmodernity admit indebtedness to Christianity, even as they despise it. One cutting-edge postmodernist, Richard Rody, says that he is glad for the 'Jewish and Christian element in our tradition that can be invoked by freeloading atheists like myself'.[5] We need to seize this gaping hole in the postmodernist position. They have a worldview that makes no sense, provides no answers and offers nothing but emptiness. This is the very opposite of Christianity. We can operate from a position of power because we possess truth.

The gospel front

The postmodern individual may be the easiest sinner in 200 years to interest in the faith. Yet he is capable of living with contradictions. He can claim to be saved and at the same time live comfortably in moral rot. He can claim to have received Jesus but not believe in his historical existence. He can claim to believe in the inerrancy of Scripture but deny absolute truth. When the gospel is presented as a means of improving self-image, giving us a spiritual and thrilling experience, providing a source for success and fulfilment, or helping us overcome loneliness, we may be speaking the language of the age; however, we have trivialized and distorted the gospel message as to make it meaningless. Groothuis warns that 'no major religious traditions — whether Buddhist, Hindu, Islamic or Jewish — has ever presented its doctrines as social constructions or as mere psychological aids to a more satisfying life. They have always been presented as truths concerning the ultimate reality and how we ought to relate to that reality.'[6]

Perhaps there has never been a time when it has been more vital to present the gospel message clearly and without apology. That Christ died on the cross to save us from our sins and give us his righteousness is the good news, which the sinner must understand. The issue on the table is sin, not felt needs. Our postmodern generation needs to hear that we have offended a holy God and are thus separated from him. If we do not tell them this we are in danger of preaching another gospel (Gal. 1:9).

Someone has said, 'In leaning over to speak to the modern world, I fear we may have fallen in.' If so, let's climb back out, open the Word and powerfully proclaim it from the housetops.

The Church's Mandate

6

Building up the Body

One of the most insightful of recent books concerning the church is actually written by an unbeliever. Alan Wolfe, a social scientist, has been observing the changing American religious scene for years. Last year he shared his research in *The Transformation of American Religion*. The message of his book is that 'religion in the United States is being transformed in radically new directions'.[1] Wolfe claims, 'Talk of Hell, damnation, and even sin has been replaced by a non-judgmental language of understanding and empathy. Gone are the arguments over doctrine and theology … More Americans than ever proclaim themselves born again in Christ, but the Lord to whom they turn rarely gets angry and frequently strengthens self-esteem. [As a result] the faithful in the United States are remarkably like everyone else.'[2]

If Wolfe's assessments are on target, what would be the catalyst for this transformation (or better stated, degeneration)? Wolfe's thesis is that in an effort to win over American culture, evangelicalism has stooped so low that it can no longer be distinguished from that culture. Take doctrine for example. Small-group Bible studies avoid theology like the plague, lest it prove divisive. Sermons are no better. 'Generally speaking, preaching in evangelically oriented growth churches, however dynamic in delivery, has remarkably little actual content. Scripture is invariably cited but only as a launching pad to reinforce the message of salvation that Jesus can offer.'[3] And what kind of salvation is Jesus offering? Why, 'Jesus will save your soul and your marriage, make you happy, heal your body, and even make you rich. Who wouldn't look twice at that offer?'[4] Nor is this a message found only in the prosperity gospel fringe. The wildly popular book *The Prayer of Jabez,* written and endorsed, not to mention read, by mainstream evangelicals, 'is a concept of religion so narcissistic that it makes prosperity theology look demanding by contrast'.[5] As a matter of fact the rapid growth of evangelicalism, as Wolfe sees it, is not due to their unique message but to their capitulation to the culture's message: 'Evangelicalism's popularity is due as much to its populistic and democratic urges — its determination to find out exactly what believers want and offer it to them — as it is to certainties of the faith.'[6] One megachurch pastor in Cincinnati describes his church growth philosophy with an 'almost' biblical quote: 'Where the Spirit of the Lord is, there is fun!'[7] And another pastor in Houston frankly admits, 'I take what is worldly, and baptize it.'[8]

These approaches are resulting in popularity. 'But popularity means bowing to, rather than resisting, popular culture, and since American popular culture is one that puts more emphasis on feeling good than thinking right, these movements tend to be especially hostile to potentially divisive doctrinal controversy.'[9] I find myself agreeing with this self-avowed unsaved man who begins to conclude his book with this statement: 'This adherence to growth can have its frustrations; watching sermons reduced to PowerPoint presentations or listening to one easily forgettable praise song after another makes one long for an evangelical willing to stand up, Luther-like, and proclaim his opposition to the latest survey of evangelical taste.'[10]

General instruction

But enough of Mr. Wolfe's penetrating analysis of evangelicalism. Alan Wolfe has skilfully exposed the mortal disease of the new paradigm church, but what is the remedy? For that we turn, not to Mr. Wolfe, but to the New Testament. And I can think of no better passage for our purposes than Ephesians 4:11-16.

What is God's design for the church? How should it function? What is its mission? The inspired apostle Paul, in a few short verses, sets the agenda. God's plan begins with gifted men whom he has given to the church (v. 11). These include apostles and prophets, who were foundational to the church, passing from the scene when that foundation had been laid (Eph. 2:20). They were followed by evangelists and pastor-teachers who build the superstructure upon the apostolic base. These gifted men are given to the church for a specific task: 'the equipping of the saints for the work of service to the building up of the body of Christ' (v. 12). This building up of the body is for the purpose of achieving four things: unity of the faith, the knowledge of the Son of God, maturity and Christ-like-ness (v. 13). In turn attaining these objectives results in God's people no longer being easily deceived, speaking the truth in love and growing up into Christ (vv. 14-15). When such lives predominate in a local church, and when the individuals of that body are living out their God-given roles, then that body of believers will be one that is both growing spiritually and being built up in love (v. 16). That's the big picture; let's now examine the details.

Specific instruction

Gifted men are given to the local church in order to 'equip the saints for the work of service'. The word 'equip' was a term used in the first century for the setting of bones. When an arm is broken, for example, the arm is out of alignment and functionally useless. The gifted men were to be instruments of God to bring proper alignment to the body in order that there might be 'the building up of the body of Christ'. In order for the body of Christ to be built up, the gifted men would need to bring about an adjustment in the local church, which would enable believers to carry out the *work of service*. How would they do this? How were they to equip the saints — what was their method? I think we can safely say that this was not to be accomplished through conducting seminars on the latest business techniques or providing psychological profiles. The instrument used for equipping was (and is) the Word of God.

This is not a logical deduction but rather clear revelation. Paul wrote to Timothy, 'All Scripture is inspired by God and profitable for teaching, for reproof, for correction, for training in righteousness; that the man of God may be adequate, *equipped* for every good work' (2 Tim. 3:16, 17, emphasis mine). The word for 'equipped' in both passages comes from the same root word *artios*, which carries the idea of equipping for a delegated task. Paul is clear in his instructions to Timothy; it is the Scriptures that equip us for every good work. So we are not surprised to find that the immediate charge to Timothy is to 'preach the word' (2 Tim. 4:1, 2). If Timothy is to equip the church he must be a preacher of the Word. And if he is to properly preach the Word he must first be one who is 'handling accurately the word of truth' (2 Tim. 2:15). That is, Timothy needed to be a careful student of the Word so that when he preached, he would be preaching the message that God intended.

This is how God proposes his church be built up — through the careful, accurate and clear preaching and teaching of his Word. Nothing else will accomplish the task. We can tell inspiring stories, sing beautiful or peppy music, fill our calendars full of social events, professionalize our program and provide small groups for every conceivable interest, but if the Scripture is not diligently, systematically and correctly taught, Christ's people will not be equipped and the body will not be built up, period. There are no exceptions to this mandate. The church must proclaim the *word of truth* — it must be the utmost priority. Congregations which focus on techniques, programs and entertainment, at the expense of the centrality of the Word, may build large followings but they will not build the church of God. Programs, drama and entertainment may amuse, soothe, inspire and stir the emotions, but they will not build Christians. Only the Word can do that.

Churches that take this instruction of the Lord seriously will be the ones marching in the direction of maturity (Eph. 4:13). Those who do not will find themselves drowning in a sea of immaturity (Eph. 4:14). These are the two options Paul lays before his readers. The first option finds the local church being equipped by the teaching of the Word and in turn building up the body of Christ. Such churches will be marked by four things. The first is unity: 'Until we all attain to the unity of the faith.' Throughout the epistles the term 'the faith' does not refer to subjective faith (e.g. 'I believe'; 'I have faith in God') but to objective truth. 'The faith' is a phrase synonymous with sound doctrine, or the body of truth as taught in the Bible. True unity is grounded in correct theology.

A certain pastor, in writing a critique of my ministry, said that he leaned toward 'unity' but I leaned toward 'purity'. That may be a true evaluation, but I do not believe there is unity without purity. An attempt at unity without doctrinal purity is merely uniformity. Many today are willing to lay down their conviction of scriptural truth in order to get along. Organizations are built under the umbrella of minimal beliefs but at the cost of great compromise, which leads to the doctrinal impurity of the church. While not all doctrinal beliefs are essential to the faith, and some are not hills worth dying on, I am amazed at what many are willing to jettison in order to embrace some form of outward unity. Paul, however, calls for a unity that is wrapped around the cardinal truths of the faith.

The second mark of the equipped church is the 'knowledge of the Son of God'. Virtually nothing is more important than our knowledge of Christ. Peter would go so far as to write, 'Seeing that His divine power has granted to us everything pertaining to life and godliness, through the true knowledge of Him who called us by His own glory and excellence' (2 Peter 1:3). If everything we need for life and godliness is found in the knowledge of Christ, why should the church dabble around with anything else? And while some, even within evangelical circles, guide us to finding Christ 'within ourselves', imagining him, or experiencing him in some mystical fashion, the fact is that the true knowledge of Christ can only be obtained through the Word. Apart from what the Scriptures say about Christ, we know nothing of absolute certainty about him.

The third and fourth marks appear to be mutually defining. We are to attain 'to a mature man', 'mature' meaning complete, not perfect. This maturity is identified as 'the measure of the stature which belongs to the fullness of Christ'. Our standard of maturity is nothing less than Christ-likeness. If we love him we will want to be like him.

Those not marching toward maturity as they are being equipped by the teaching of the Word are left hopelessly entangled in a web of immaturity (Eph. 4:14). Unfortunately, the description given of the immature believer hits very close to home in our evangelical environment today. As Paul portrays the immature believer (or church), the one not equipped by the teaching of the Word, he uses the illustration of a child. The proof of a child's immaturity is found in two characteristics found in all children.

They are unstable: 'We are no longer to be children, tossed here and there by waves.' Children are notoriously fickle and changeable. They lack self-control; are creatures of extremes and are ruled by their emotions. So too, immature Christians are on emotional, spiritual and doctrinal roller coasters. The day after a church retreat they are ready to follow the Lord anywhere; by Wednesday all enthusiasm is gone. While attending a Christian musical concert they are overflowing with feelings of love and warmth for the Lord and others. The next morning they don't 'feel' like reading the Scriptures or praying and so they don't. When convicted of sin, they make strong pledges of future obedience. But a few days later they buckle under the same old temptations. They have mastered the art of selective obedience to Christ. Their faith, while possibly genuine, is superficial, lacking substance and power. They are truly 'tossed here and there by waves' — at the mercy of so many influences, fads, powerful personalities and temptations that float into their lives.

They are easily deceived: 'And carried about by every wind of doctrine, by the trickery of men, by craftiness in deceitful scheming.' Baby Christians remain such because they are constantly being deceived. Rather than being equipped by the Word, these immature believers are taken in by false doctrines, con-artists and slick programs and campaigns. Place in front of them a great communicator and they lack the discernment to filter his message. Baby Christians are always chasing after the latest book or message promising them instant spirituality.

What is the remedy to this endless merry-go-round of childishness? 'Speaking the truth in love' (v. 15). We need to keep the context in mind. Paul is not calling for open and honest communication, although that is a biblical teaching and supported in verse

25. At this point he is giving us the antidote to spiritual immaturity and that antidote is found in 'equipping the saints for the work of service' (v. 12). Udo Middelmann admonishes:

> The church has lost the wider audience because it gave up much of what it should know and in the past was good at: the light shed on human reality from the Word of God in love, encouragement, moral clarity, and compassion... When the church abandons her singular calling, she is usually not even very good in the attempt to compete with the street and market.[11]

The church must concentrate on its mandate to equip the saints and not be sidetracked by other things. As the body is built up through the careful teaching of the Word of God by the gifted men and the application of that truth by the local church, the body 'grow[s] up in all aspects into Him, who is the Head, even Christ'. The loving communication of God's truth is what matures lives and develops godly churches. Verse sixteen tells us that it is the power of Christ working through the members of the body functioning as God designs, which ultimately causes the growth of the body.

We ignore God's plan as outlined in Ephesians 4:11-16 for the growth of the body of Christ at great peril. If we want churches that please people, then our priority is to listen to the strategy of people. But if we desire churches that please God, surely we will want to know and implement God's methodology. Whom we listen to reveals whom we want to please.

Church Discipline and Church Growth

Undoubtedly the most neglected and misunderstood activity that any church can undertake is that of disciplining its members. Our society equates love with tolerance. 'Live and let live' is its mantra; 'What right do you have to judge me?' is our challenge. These attitudes, of course, have infiltrated the minds of Christians. Couple that with the fact that most Christians have never witnessed biblically-based church discipline and we can readily understand why even solid believers are unnerved at the mere mention of the 'D' word. Nor am I aware of any church growth seminars espousing discipline as a means to draw the masses. As a matter of fact, church discipline is antithetical to the seeker-sensitive movement since a goal of church discipline is purity, which is not an attractive feature to most unbelievers and even many Christians. It should, therefore, give us serious reason for reflection when we realize that past generations considered church discipline one of the marks of the true church. Certainly discipline has been abused in the past and biblical guidelines have been often ignored, but discipline has always been a characteristic of the church. It is our generation that is out of step with both the historic church and with the teachings of Scripture. What has brought about this alteration in the modern church? There are two culprits, as I see it: lack of biblical instruction concerning church discipline and a modified view of sin.

Whatever happened to sin?

When the mayor of Washington, D.C., is arrested for cocaine possession, he immediately checks into a treatment center, thereby
suggesting that he is not guilty so much as sick. When one of
baseball's greatest stars is charged with gambling on the sport, he
tells the nation that he has 'a problem', compulsive gambling, a
sickness. When a gunman kills three children on a school ground,
rather than call the ministers of the nearest churches, the principal
calls professional therapists to assist the children in dealing with
their fears. When the press reveals that a minister has been arrested for an indecent act in a public place, he immediately enters
a therapeutic center in a distant state for the treatment of stress,
while his superiors in the church explain the burdens he has been
carrying in ministry.[1]

　　Sin has been airbrushed out of the minds and hearts of Western society as well as the church. What the Bible calls sin we now
call sickness, disorders, phobias and syndromes. This is more than
semantics; it is a fundamental change in the understanding of human nature and the human condition. According to Scripture,
mankind's great problem is that they are fallen creatures; they are
totally depraved — incapable, unwilling and unable to please God
and live holy lives (Rom. 3:10-18; Eph. 2:1-3). What sinners need
is not to feel better about themselves, but to be born again (2 Cor.
5:17). They need their sins forgiven (Eph. 1:7), the righteousness
of God placed on their account (2 Cor. 5:21) and the transforming
power of the Holy Spirit in their lives (Gal. 5:16, 22-25). New believers now find themselves (hopefully) in a nurturing local body of
Christ; they have at their disposal the very words of God in the Bible and the Holy Spirit is powerfully at work in their hearts. Still the
battle with the flesh rages (Gal. 5:17-21), the devil seeks to devour
(1 Peter 5:8) and the world ever calls to conformity (1 John 2:15-
17). Under such conditions casualties of war are to be expected,
so no one is shocked to hear that Christians sin. God made provi-
sion for regular forgiveness through the confession of those sins (1
John 1:9) and repentance (2 Cor. 7:9, 10). In addition, means for
victory over sin is found in laying aside our old self with its sinful
practices, renewal in the spirit of our mind and putting on the new

self (Eph. 5:22-24). Contrary to popular opinion, the message of Scripture, in all of its simplicity and directness, is quite positive: we are sinners, but sinners can be forgiven, and through the power of the Word and the Holy Spirit we can live in a manner 'worthy of [our] calling' (Eph. 4:1).

All of this changes, however, when mankind's great problem is misdiagnosed. If we are sick, we don't need forgiveness but medical attention. If we are victims of disorders we don't need forgiveness but behavioural modification. If we are a mass of unmet emotional needs we don't need forgiveness but someone or something to meet our needs. The packaging of the gospel, as well as our Christian lives, largely depends upon our understanding of the human condition. Having drunk at the well of secular psychology for decades now, many Christians and churches have lost the concept of man as sinner, and have embraced the concept of man as victim. If we are victims we don't need to confess sin because we are not at fault. Instead the blame is passed elsewhere. Anna Russell's 'Psychiatric Folk Song' captures this concept well:

> I went to my psychiatrist to be psychoanalyzed
> To find out why I killed the cat and blacked my husband's eye.
> He laid me on a downy couch to see what he could find,
> And here's what he dredged up, from my subconscious mind.
> When I was one, my mummy hid my dolly in a trunk
> And so it follows, naturally, that I am always drunk.
> When I was two, I saw my father kiss the maid one day,
> And that is why I suffer from kleptomania.
> At three I had a feeling of ambivalence towards my brothers.
> And so it follows naturally I poisoned all my lovers.
> But I am happy now I have learned the lessons this has taught:
> Everything I do that's wrong, is someone else's fault![2]

It is no wonder that one observer lamented, 'Sin really has disappeared from the pulpit. It's too much of a downer, I'm afraid.'

Simply because the Christian community has renamed or reclassified sin as something more docile does not mean that the essence of sin has actually changed. If your doctor diagnosed you with cancer, but in order not to alarm you he tells you your problem is indigestion and prescribes Pepto-Bismol, he has done you a disservice. As uncomfortable as it might be, identifying your illness is the first step toward treatment. We can rename sin but ultimately we are only fooling ourselves and pandering to our own self-deception, leaving us vulnerable to sin's destructive power.

The importance of a proper knowledge of sin is illustrated by a story told of Martin Luther and a man who was seeking an opportunity to stab the Reformer. Luther had received a portrait of the would-be murderer, so that, wherever he went, he was on his guard against the assassin. Using this as an illustration, Luther said, 'God knows that there are sins that would destroy us, and he has therefore given us portraits of them in his Word, so that, wherever we see them, we may say, "That is a sin that would stab me; I must beware of that evil thing, and keep out of its way."'[3]

What the modern church is having a hard time grasping these days is that people really are sinners. And because we are sinners, despite the work of the Spirit and the Scriptures, even saints are drawn to the deeds of the flesh. Renaming those deeds something more palpable does not solve the problem. D. A. Carson warns:

> People do not drift toward holiness. Apart from grace-driven effort, people do not gravitate toward godliness, prayer, obedience to Scripture, faith and delight in the Lord. We drift toward disobedience and call it freedom; we drift toward superstition and call it faith. We cherish the indiscipline of lost self-control and call it relaxation; we slouch toward prayerlessness and delude ourselves into thinking we have escaped legalism; we slide toward godlessness and convince ourselves we have been liberated.[4]

Church discipline

What desperately needs to be reclaimed by Christ's church today is a biblical concept of sin and sin's potential power in a believer's life. When it is once again recognized that the flesh, which houses the principle of sin, is our great enemy we will once again be ready to do battle with the weapons that God has provided. One of those weapons is church discipline. To be sure this is not the first step in dealing with sin — it is the last. Normally our sin issues are handled on a personal and private level as we confess our sins to God and seek forgiveness from others. It is very rare for the local church to have to step forward and deal publicly with the sins of God's people. Unfortunately, there will be occasions when this action will be necessary, so our Lord has provided us with guidelines for those situations. The Scriptures clearly outline the goals, reasons and steps related to church discipline.

Goals of church discipline

There are a number of purposes for church discipline, but it must first be stated that the aim is not to inflict punishment on the offender. The church is not seeking vengeance; that is God's prerogative (Rom. 12:19). It is not spitefully trying to teach a lesson. Discipline should not spring from angry, mean-spirited hearts. As a matter of fact, unless a church is deeply grieved and sorrowful over a fallen brother or sister I do not believe that the church is in a spiritual position to deal with sin within its ranks. Discipline must spring from hearts of love and compassion.

This being the case, what are the biblical goals of discipline? First, the goal of all church discipline should be the restoration of the sinner. Galatians 6:1 says it best: 'Brethren, even if a man is caught in any trespass, you who are spiritual restore such a one in the spirit of gentleness; each one looking to yourself, lest you too be tempted.' When individuals are removed from the church it is for the purpose of reclaiming them for Christ. The objective is not to rid ourselves of a troublesome person — to wash our hands of a tough situation and move on. It is to impress upon Christians the gravity of their sin so as to cause them to fall on their knees before the Lord in heart-felt repentance. This is the first step towards restoring this individual to godly fellowship with the Lord.

Not only has sin resulted in broken joyful fellowship with the Lord, but it has also resulted in alienation from God's people. Therefore, reconciliation is the next goal of church discipline. It is interesting to find that in Matthew 18, one of the most important passages on this subject, the motivation for reproving a brother in sin is that if he listens, 'you have won your brother' (v. 15).

While restoration and reconciliation are the desired result for the one in sin, the purity of the local body of Christ and its protection from contamination is equally important. When the apostle Paul called for church discipline of the immoral man in 1 Corinthians 5, he rebuked the church for allowing this man to remain in their fellowship. He asked them, 'Do you not know that a little leaven leavens the whole lump of dough?' Then he commanded them to 'clean out the old leaven'. They had apparently congratulated themselves on their loving tolerance of this sinful situation, but Paul was not impressed. They had allowed this adulterous relationship to continue within their fellowship not realizing that the pollution of the body was the result. When sin is ignored or tolerated, even in the name of love, it sends the message that sin is not of any great significance. The result is an impure church and a watered-down message.

Reasons for church discipline

In the New Testament we are given examples and commands to discipline unrepentant Christians for a number of specific sins. The best known example is the immorality found in 1 Corinthians 5. Concerning this professed Christian man Paul tells the church to remove him from the fellowship (v. 2). This involved more than a paper transaction — more than a simple removal of his name from the membership roles, or even from the times of worship and fellowship. Church discipline would involve a powerful spiritual transaction in which this man living in open unconfessed sin would actually be 'delivered … to Satan for the destruction of his flesh, that his spirit may be saved in the day of the Lord Jesus'. By removing the individual from the body he was now placed in the world system, the domain of Satan himself. Here, outside of the protection of the church, he was fair game for the devil. The goal of this action was that the man would see his sin and turn to Christ.

Similar action is to be taken in the case of doctrinal heresy. In 1 Timothy 1:10 we find Paul delivering Hymenaeus and Alexander over to Satan in order to teach them not to blaspheme, which in the context had reference to rejection of the faith. Later in 2 Timothy 2:18 the particular doctrinal heresy of these men has to do with false teaching concerning the resurrection. Unless such men are publicly rebuked, their false doctrines will spread like gangrene (2:17). Of course Paul is not referencing minor doctrinal differences among Christians, but when the cardinal doctrines of the faith are under attack there can be no compromise.

Removal from the church is also espoused for repeated divisiveness. In Titus 3:10 we are told to reject a factious man after a first and second warning. In passages such as 2 Thessalonians 3, the causes for church discipline are broadened to include public, unconfessed and wilful sins of any type. Verse six calls on us 'to keep aloof from every brother who leads an unruly life and not according to the traditions which you received from us'. Then after a discussion of Christians who refused to work for their living, Paul concludes, 'And if anyone does not obey our instruction in this letter, take special note of that man and do not associate with him, so that he may be put to shame. And yet do not regard him as an enemy, but admonish him as a brother' (vv. 14-15). 1 Corinthians 5:11-13 sums it up well: 'I wrote to you not to associate with any so-called brother if he should be an immoral person, or covetous, or an idolater, or a reviler, or a drunkard, or a swindler — not even to eat with such a one … Remove the wicked man from among yourselves.'

It should be understood that the Scripture is not calling for sanctified witch-hunts where everyone lives in mortal fear of slipping up and facing removal from the church. Those who are disciplined are not the ones who struggle with the flesh, losing some battles, confessing their sin and moving on for Christ. That is a description of all believers. Discipline is reserved for those who have chosen to sin, are living an ungodly lifestyle, and are refusing to confess, truly repent and live lives that evidence repentance. These are individuals who claim to be Christians but thumb their noses at their Lord with our actions. After repeated attempts to call them to walk with Christ they have refused, and now live what Paul calls an unruly life.

Steps to church discipline

Most consider Matthew 18:15-20 the best explanation of the steps that need to be taken when dealing with a person in sin. This is probably wise, but it should be noted that when these words of our Lord were spoken, the church, as a New Testament body of Christ had not yet been formed, although his words anticipate that it soon would be. In addition, the epistles, which explain New Testament living, never repeat these steps although Titus 3:10 comes very close. It should also be noted in the examples given above we have no indication that the Matthew 18 formula was followed. This may be because Jesus appears to be dealing with private sins against an individual rather than known public sins, although this cannot be dogmatically stated. There is no necessity for me to go privately to discuss the moral failure of a Christian who is openly living with someone who is not his wife. The first step of Matthew 18 could be skipped in this case and step 2 or 3 be initiated. We see this pattern in Paul's rebuke of Peter in Galatians 2, and in his public pronouncement of the man in immorality in 1 Corinthians 5.

Still, as a general rule Matthew serves us well, for when we see a brother in sin (whether they have sinned against us or not), as concerned Christians we should personally, or with others, approach the errant fellow believer and reprove him (v. 15). By God's grace your brother may listen to this kind rebuke, taking appropriate action to deal with his sin. Fortunately, the vast majority of sin issues are solved on this level, but occasionally it becomes necessary to go to the next stage in which two or more 'witnesses' get involved. This step is for 'confirming the fact' of the sin. It is possible that at this juncture the witnesses will see the situation differently. Perhaps the one reproving has his facts twisted. Possibly there is a misunderstanding rather than a sin. The witnesses, who should be godly people, are to sort this out and determine the facts of the matter. If it is determined that the individual is indeed in sin, they are to call him to repentance. If this call is rejected, the small group is to tell it to the church.

There is some difference of opinion at this point as to what this means. Is the whole church informed or just the spiritual leadership? Either way the church is now to call this brother to repentance. It is only after the church has been spurned that the final step of church discipline takes place. Jesus said that such a one is now to 'be to you as a Gentile, and tax-gatherer' (v. 17).

When we compare this statement with 1 Corinthians 5:11 — 'I wrote to you not to associate with any so-called brother...', 2 Thessalonians 3:14b-15 — 'Do not associate with him, so that he may be put to shame. And yet do not regard him as an enemy, but admonish him as a brother', and Galatians 6:1 — 'You who are spiritual, restore such a one in the spirit of gentleness', we come away with a clearer picture of what Jesus is demanding. We are not to shun, deprecate or treat unkindly those under discipline. But we must not fellowship, worship or socialize (*not even eat with such a one*) with them. The goal is not to inflict harm but to impress upon them the gravity of their sin and consequences of rebellion against their God, and to maintain the purity of the church. The objective, once again, is restoration.

Conclusion

In the growth-at-any-cost mindset of the modern church, discipline is foreign and distasteful. 'Churches have become hospitals where sin-sick souls are given aspirin and entertainment to distract them from the diseases of their souls. God forgive us, we are more concerned with numbers than with holiness.'[5] Christians determined to please God will see the value and importance of church discipline in our efforts to shepherd God's people.

8

Love for an Offensive Gospel

Virtually all students of the Scriptures would agree that the church exists *not only for the corporate worship of God, but also for evangelism and edification.* We are called to share the gospel with lost souls (Rom. 10:14) and to disciple those who come to Christ (Matt. 28:19). Edification takes place as the local church gathers together to be taught the Word and to minister to one another (Eph. 4:11-16; 1 Cor. 12). Evangelism is to take place in the community as the church scatters (Matt. 28:19, 20; Rom. 10:14). In the New Testament the members of a local church are never seen coming together for the purpose of evangelism. Evangelism took place apart from the meetings of the church — in the workplace, at the synagogue, in town squares, among family members and friends. The early Christian went to where the unbelievers were and presented the gospel of Christ. They did not necessarily do this through evangelistic blitzes on Thursday nights — this wasn't necessary. Everyone had their pool of opportunity through the normal discourse of their lives, just as most of us do today.

One thing they did not do, to our knowledge, was invite unbelievers to their church services in order to evangelize them. The closest we get to any kind of evangelism within the context of church services is 1 Corinthians 14:23-25: 'If therefore the whole church should assemble together and ... all prophesy, and an unbeliever or an ungifted man enters, he is convicted by all, he is called to account by all; the secrets of his heart are disclosed; and so he will fall on his face and worship God, declaring that God is certainly among you.'

The obvious implication is that the Corinthian church had gathered for the purpose of mutual edification — evangelism is not on the stated agenda. No evangelistic sermon is preached; the music is not geared toward the interests of unbelievers; spiritual language is not tempered to keep from offending or confusing the unsaved; absolutely nothing is done with the 'seeking' unbeliever in mind. But, if an unbeliever happens to show up and hears the truth of God expounded and watches as the body functions, he may very well have his heart opened and be drawn to Christ. This is a wonderful collateral result of the church functioning in a biblical manner, but it is not the reason that the church assembles. *That evangelism can take place when the church is gathered is not in question, but biblically, evangelism is not the primary focus when the local body of Christ gathers for worship and edification.*

With this New Testament foundation in mind it should give us great concern when we find the philosophy behind the church-growth, or seeker-sensitive, movement ignoring this pattern and developing churches that have structured their regular services for the purpose of evangelizing the lost. This movement has turned the church on its head as the main services of the church have been transformed into evangelistic outreaches. Most churches adopting this philosophy have relegated edification and instructional services for believers to mid-week gatherings or small groups. Yet, these services tend to be basic in nature as well, geared towards keeping the new convert happy and coming. Even Charles Finney, who in many respects is the great-grandfather of the market-driven church, warned way back in the mid 1800s:

> If men enter upon the Christian life only for gain in the line of their hopes and fears, you must keep up the influence of these considerations, and must expect to work upon these only; that is, you must expect to have selfish Christians and a selfish church ... [They will say] we became Christians ... only for the sake of promoting our own interest, and we have nothing to do in the Christian life on any other motive.[1]

In other words, whatever you used to bring them in must be continued or they will leave.[2] If you enticed people to attend your church on Sunday morning through great entertainment, promises of met felt needs, or material prosperity, you will have a very difficult time 'switching horses' on Wednesday night and offering them a solid diet of biblical exposition. They did not come in the front door to learn the Scriptures and worship God. They were drawn by a good show, promises of success, personal fulfilment and happiness. If you are to keep them coming you must give them more of the same.

This is the dilemma that many churches now face. So why do they put themselves in this position? Because they do not believe that people will respond to the gospel unless it is presented in a winsome package that connects positively with their felt needs. D. A. Carson laments:

> It is hard, for instance, to deny the influence of pluralism on evangelical preachers who increasingly reconstruct the 'gospel' along the lines of felt needs, knowing that such a presentation will be far better appreciated than one that articulates truth with hard edges (i.e., that insists that certain contrary things are false), or that warns of the wrath to come. How far can such reconstruction go before what is preached is no longer the gospel in any historical or biblical sense?[3]

An example

Recently I picked up a bulletin from a local evangelical church that offers a good example of the realization of Carson's fears. At the bottom of the sermon note's handout was the plan of salvation which was in essence a watered-down version of the 'Four Spiritual Laws'. Here are the supposed four steps to salvation:

> God loves you and has a plan for your life.
> We make mistakes and decisions that don't please God.
> Jesus died on the cross for all the 'bad stuff'

You can accept His forgiveness, follow Jesus and become
   a Christian through prayer.

There are numerous problems with these steps but the most
glaring is the absence of any mention of sin. Sin is sand-blasted out
of this statement and replaced with 'mistakes', 'decisions that don't
please God' and 'bad stuff'. Why would this evangelical church,
one which places evangelism at the top of its priority list, want to
shy so far away from using the word 'sin'? And why, when it attempts to use synonyms as substitutes for sin, does it choose to use
words that do not define sin? Mistakes, decisions that don't please
God and 'bad stuff' are lame alternatives for the biblical concept
of sin. Rebelliousness, disobedience, transgressions, iniquity, evil
or wickedness might have been decent stand-ins, but not mistakes.
Christ did not die on the cross because we make bad choices or
mistakes. He died because we were helpless, ungodly sinners who
happened to also be the very enemies of God (Rom. 5:6-10). And
we don't become Christians by asking God to forgive our mistakes,
we become Christians when, after recognizing our lost condition,
we by faith repent and receive Jesus Christ and the gift of God's
saving grace (John 1:12; Eph. 2:1-10).

What would provoke an evangelical, evangelistic-minded
church to so alter the gospel message as to gut it of, as Carson says,
'its historical and biblical sense'? Almost certainly their motivation
is a noble one — the desire to see people become saved. But they
fear that very few will respond to a gospel which calls sin, sin and
identifies unbelievers as ungodly, rebellious enemies of God. With
Robert Schuller they apparently suppose, 'Once a person believes
he is an "unworthy sinner", it is doubtful if he can really honestly
accept the saving grace God offers in Jesus Christ.'[4] Such Christian
leaders simply do not believe that the unaltered gospel message, as
presented in Scripture, will draw the lost to Christ. It is too offensive, too degrading, and too foolish to be appetizing. If we are to
entice unbelievers to Christ, we must somehow make the foolishness of the cross attractive to sinners.

Proclaiming an offensive message

There is nothing new to this approach — it is as old as the New Testament. The apostle Paul apparently was under the same pressure to produce converts. Some at Corinth seemed to be leaning on Paul to preach a gospel-lite message that would incorporate some of the in-vogue wisdom so popular among unbelievers in the first century. At the very least Paul should not be so offensive — he was turning everyone off, Jew and Gentile alike, by insistence on the centrality of the cross. What was Paul to do? I Corinthians 1:18-30 is the answer. Verse eighteen sets the stage: 'For the word of the cross is to those who are perishing foolishness, but to us who are being saved it is the power of God.' Our perspective on the gospel is determined exclusively by our relationship with the Saviour. To the lost the good news is foolish; to the redeemed it is the power of God.

It is of utmost importance that we wrestle with the truth that the unbeliever views the cross as foolish. This being the case, in our attempts to evangelize there appears to be two options. We can present the gospel exactly as Scripture describes, knowing that its message will repulse the unbeliever devoid of the enlightening ministry of the Spirit (2 Cor. 3:17-18; 4:6). Or we can attempt to make the gospel 'unfoolish' by altering the message enough to make it sound enticing to unregenerate minds. That is, we can make them an offer they can't refuse. Before we embark too enthusiastically on this second option we might want to examine how Paul, under the inspiration of the Holy Spirit, sought to resolve the dilemma.

In 1 Corinthians 1 verses 22 and 23 Paul affirms that what the unsaved person seeks is foreign to the gospel. In the culture of Paul's lifetime Jews asked for signs, while Greeks searched for wisdom. This being the case a sharp marketer would surely give his audience what they wanted. He would deemphasize the negative and accentuate the positive. For the Jews he would give evidence of the signs they wanted. For the Greeks he would reason philosophically, proving that receiving Christ and living for God was the only reasonable choice for wise men. It is interesting that

Paul could have legitimately done either one of these things. Christ gave signs of his deity and Messiah-ship and certainly Christianity makes sense. But Paul saw clearly that the danger lay in the temptation to filter out anything that might offend his audience. To be true to the gospel this temptation would not only have to be resisted, but the actual offensive part of the good news would need to be emphasized. This emphasis was not for the purpose of intentionally stepping on toes — Paul would go out of his way not to offend unnecessarily his unsaved audience — as he would say later in this same epistle (9:19-23). But he understood that to tamper with the central essence of the gospel, in order to attract a wider audience, was not just to diminish its power but to so alter its message as to create 'a different gospel' altogether (Gal. 1:6).

The central piece of the gospel, which was so offensive to the Corinthians, was the cross. This is a bit hard for us to grasp today since we have sentimentalized the cross, making it into a piece of jewellery and decoration for our walls, rather than a symbol of death. The stigma of the cross is largely lost to our generation, but in the first century it bore very different, even disgraceful connotations. The Roman Empire reserved crucifixion for three classes of people: rebellious slaves, the worst of criminals and defeated foes of the empire.[5] Gentiles, therefore, viewed crucified men with disdain and contempt. 'This animosity toward crucified men was deeply engraved on the social consciousness of the world to which Paul brought his message about a crucified Savior.'[6] To the Gentiles the crucifixion was pure foolishness, madness, craziness. Who could imagine that God's Son dying on a cross as a common criminal would be pivotal to God's redemption plan?

For the Jew things were even worse. 'Though Gentiles viewed crucifixion as a punishment reserved for detestable people ... the Jews believed the victim was cursed by God (cf. Deuteronomy 21:23). Consequently, the stigma went beyond social disgrace to a declaration of God's spiritual judgment against the victim.'[7] According to the Jewish mindset Jesus not only died a despicable death, but he was also cursed of God. How could he be the Messiah, the Saviour, and be under the curse of God? The crucifixion would prove to be a 'stumbling block' (1 Cor. 1:23) to the Jews.

The Greek word translated 'stumbling block' is *skandalon* (from which we get our word 'scandal') and refers to an enticement to apostasy and unbelief.

> In other words, the spiritual offense of the cross actually worked to make some Jews go astray. Remarkably, the crucifixion — so essential to eternal life — actually hindered Jews from coming to saving faith. They simply could not overcome their preconceived notions about the significance of crucifixion ... The very content of Paul's message caused Jews to turn away.[8]

Paul was not ignorant of the fact that the preaching of a crucified Saviour would more than dull the attractiveness of the gospel; it would be a major impediment. Before his audience could get to the good news of forgiveness of sin and reconciliation with God, they had to first come to the cross, which was abhorrent to them. But this did not deter Paul from preaching the centrality of the cross, for to the 'called' the crucified Christ is 'the power of God and the wisdom of God' (1 Cor. 1:24). The good news is grounded in the cross; to eliminate it, or even to minimize it, would be to rob the gospel of its power to save.

In the twenty-first century this particular debate seems very distant. The cross, as most envision it today, is more likely to elicit warm fuzzies than disgust or revulsion. Still Paul's point is not lost. The gospel continues to offend. Whether it is the crucifixion itself, insistence on recognizing our sins and repenting, receiving by faith One that we have never seen, or abandoning our self-reliance, denying ourselves, taking up our cross, and following him — the gospel offends (Matt. 16:24). None of these things pander to our ego. The gospel is not a message about how to get ahead in life, or how to find the key to happiness and success. Paul stayed focused on what was true and essential and he would not be moved by the pressures around him. '"Christ crucified" was not a "seeker-friendly" message in the first century. It was an absurd obscenity to Gentiles and a scandalous oxymoron to Jews. The gospel guaranteed offense.'[9] Paul's example should encourage us today to not sell out the gospel for perceived evangelistic success. We need to stand by the message given in the New Testament, proclaim it with authority and let God give the increase (1 Cor. 3:6-7).

The Scriptures

9

The Use and Misuse of Scripture

The truly blessed individual is described in Psalm 1: 'His delight is in the Law of the Lord, and in His Law he meditates day and night.' Godly people delight in the Word of God. They love it, they cherish it, and they can't get enough of it. That is why they meditate on it day and night. It is their joy to contemplate God's truth. Such lovers of truth take seriously Paul's injunction to 'be diligent to present yourself approved to God as a workman who does not need to be ashamed, handling accurately the word of truth' (2 Tim. 2:15). Those who desire God's approval must handle accurately, or literally, 'cut straight', the word of truth. They must diligently study the Bible in order to interpret it correctly and then apply it properly. Anything less results in workers who are ashamed — not because they do not mean well, or do not love the Lord, but because they have mishandled the Scriptures and thus, at least to some degree, live false lives, leading possibly even to the dishonouring of God. No child of God wants to dishonour his Lord and so the diligent study of the Word is serious business. We do not have the option of carelessness or superficiality, much less distortion of the biblical text. So it is the precious privilege of the child of God to grow in his understanding of Scripture year by year. Never perfectly, but always earnestly, the believer craves to increasingly know God's truth more fully. For in doing so, we honour Him and live life abundantly (John 10:10).

Of course, those who so love the glorious truths of the Word will also 'contend earnestly for the faith' (the body of truth found in the Word) 'which was once for all delivered to the saints' (Jude 3). All of us will fight for the things we treasure. If we treasure our marriage, we will stand against all obstacles that would destroy that marriage. If we value our children, we will protect and guard them from all that would harm them. If we adore the Word of God, how can we do anything less than fight for it against all adversaries? It has always been beyond my comprehension as to how a believer can claim to love God's Word and yet tolerate teachers who pervert it.

This brings us to the topic of this chapter. Satan, of course, has always sought to twist and misrepresent the Scriptures. Over the years he has invented many ways of doing so, but recently he has used several seemingly benign methods that I believe are going undetected by many evangelical Christians. Please consider two areas with me in this chapter that need careful evaluation.

Hermeneutics

Hermeneutics is the science that teaches the principles, laws and methods of interpretation. Whenever we attempt to interpret anything, be it the tax code, the sports page, a novel or the Bible we use certain hermeneutical methods. When we seek to understand almost any literature, besides the Bible, we all tend to use normal, literal hermeneutics. Loosely this means that we take words and sentences at face value, expecting that the author meant what he said and we can understand what he meant. Theologians call this the grammatical-historical approach. But when it comes to the Bible, Christians throughout history have had a hard time using normal hermeneutics. Instead they have tried to infuse into the Word meanings that were never intended. For a fuller understanding of some of the errant approaches of the past, see my book, *'I Just Wanted More Land', Jabez*, or Bernard Ramm's *Protestant Biblical Interpretation*.

I am more interested at this point in some of the newer approaches that are rapidly becoming popular among the evangelical elite. Some of the new hermeneutics seem to spring from postmodern and deconstruction thought. But whether or not this is the case, there is a movement away from the objective grammatical-historical method to a more subjective slant in which the reader's understanding of the text takes precedence over the original intent of the author (in the case of the Bible, the Holy Spirit). On a popular level this is evident in the many Bible studies in which believers are encouraged to share what a certain passage of Scripture 'means to me'. Often no one has actually done any careful study of the text, nor is anyone's interpretation considered wrong or challenged. The implication is that whatever the text means to you is a proper interpretation, even if it is far from what the author intended it to mean.

On the scholarly front the rage is to back-pedal from the grammatical-historical approach and develop methods that emphasize the subjective element (i.e., what it means to me). Some scholars effectively neutralize the meaning of the text by bringing a pre-understanding to it. Rather than allowing the text to speak for itself, a preconceived foreign meaning is brought to the passage with the result that the true meaning is lost or distorted. For example, open theists bring to the text of Scripture a preconceived understanding that God cannot know the future with certainty. They then reinterpret any passage which speaks of God's foreknowledge through the grid of their presuppositions. Others, even in conservative camps, are advocating that a passage of Scripture can have multiple meanings. This is a repudiation of one of the cardinal rules of grammatical-historical hermeneutics, that of one meaning in any given text. This is a vast and concerning subject, far beyond the scope of this study. I would refer you to Robert Thomas' excellent book, *Evangelical Hermeneutics*, for more on this matter. The bottom line is that if we desert normal methods of interpretation, if we do not allow the text to speak for itself, and if we insist on bringing our own meanings to the passage, we will not be accurately handling the Word of God. Rather we must use principles of hermeneutics drawn from the Bible itself to determine our interpretation of Scripture.

Translations

Flowing directly from the stream of modern hermeneutics are modern translations. I have explored some of the issues surrounding

translations, including the King James controversies and the man-
uscripts debate, in other places, so I will not replow that ground. At
this point I am more interested in the philosophy behind the numerous translations of Scripture available today. Most translations
in the past have been attempts to render into another language
(my comments will be limited to English) as closely as possible the
Hebrew and Greek words in which the Bible was originally written.
While no translation has ever been infallible (only the original au-
tographs are), and while all translations involve a certain amount
of interpretation — since it is impossible to literally render word for
word Hebrew and Greek into English — most translations attempted to stay as close as possible to the biblical languages. The *King
James Version* is a case in point. The translators endeavoured to
produce a translation of Scripture that was as literal as possible and
still be readable. That they did a remarkable job can be attested by
the longevity of the KJV, first published in 1611 and still being read
today (with some modifications) by millions. Other works such as
the *American Standard Version* (ASV), *The New American Standard Bible* (NASB), the *New King James* (NKJV) and now the *English Standard Version* (ESV), have all had this same philosophy
and all, I believe, are excellent attempts at translations.

But hand in glove with the rise of subjective hermeneutics has
been the popularity of translations that do not attempt a word-
for-word, literal translation, but a thought for thought rendering.
These freer translations aim at dynamic equivalence: producing
the same effect on today's reader that the original text produced on
the original reader. In such versions far more interpretation on the
part of the translators goes into the work as they attempt to explain
what the authors meant rather than rendering what they said and
allowing the reader to interpret the words for themselves. To some
degree this is true of any translation, but the freer the translation
the more interpretation is taking place by the translators. Easily the
best known translation in this field is the *New International Version*,
which has become the best selling English Bible of our times. Recently the *Today's New International Version* has been published.
It attempts a gender-neutral translation — replacing masculine pro-
nouns and sometimes nouns in an effort to make the Bible less

offensive to certain segments of society. Also popular is the *New Living Translation*.

Then there are the paraphrases such as *The Living Bible* and more recently, *The Message*, which make no attempt to translate words at all but amount to running commentaries on the Bible. Understood as mere commentaries, paraphrases may have their place. Unfortunately, as we will see, many misconstrue them to be translations leading to a plethora of problems.

The bottom line is that the further a translation moves from the literal, the more interpretation is taking place, and the words are less accurate to the original text. Let me give you a typical example. Observe the translation of the Greek word *sarx* in a number of translations. It is important to note that *sarx* literally means 'flesh' and can refer to physical flesh or something spiritual, depending on the context. Compare five versions' rendering of *sarx* in Romans 8:9a:

> **KJV**: 'But you are not in the flesh, but in the Spirit, if so be that the Spirit of God dwells in you.'

> **NASB**: 'However, you are not in the flesh but in the Spirit if indeed the Spirit of God dwells in you.'

> **NIV**: 'You, however, are controlled not by your sinful nature but by the Spirit, if the Spirit of God lives in you.'

> **LB**: 'But you are not like that. You are controlled by your new nature if you have the Spirit of God living in you.'

> **The Message**: 'But if God himself has taken up residence in your life, you can hardly be thinking more of yourselves than of him.'

Note that the first two translations — both literal in philosophy — translate the word *sarx* as 'flesh', leaving the interpretation of the word up to the reader. Also, the literal rendering of the sentence produces the sense that if the Holy Spirit dwells in an individual, then they are not in the flesh. In other words, a person cannot be a believer and still be 'in the flesh'. The Christian's position in Christ is that they are no longer in the flesh. But the NIV translates *sarx* as 'controlled not by your sinful nature'. Not only is one Greek word translated by a phrase, but that phrase changes the meaning of the text. The NIV interpretation would lead us to believe that the issue is one of control, not one of position. It is not, according to the NIV, that we have been set free from the flesh (i.e., we are no longer in the flesh) but that we are not controlled by our sinful nature. A massive amount of interpretation has taken place, and the interpretation actually changes the meaning of the verse from Paul's intent. *The Living Bible* rendering goes further, completely removing any idea of the flesh at all. Now we are controlled by our new nature — a concept foreign to the passage. What *The Message* is doing is anyone's guess, and quite typical of this paraphrase. *The Message's* message is a complete distortion of the text. It is amazing the accolades that this paraphrase has received in the Christian community when it consistently changes the meaning of the Scriptures.

The point is this — the further a translation moves from the philosophy of literalness, the less the work is a translation and the more it is an interpretation, and the more untrustworthy it becomes. Dynamic-equivalent versions are usually easier to read and therefore may be helpful to young Christians and children. They also may prove useful as reference tools and general reading, but for serious Bible study a literal translation is indispensable.

10

The Purpose-Driven Life: An Evaluation

Because of the hermeneutical and translation issues found in the previous chapter, we have a logical and grave concern. If the reader is free to alter the meaning of the objective biblical text due to his own subjectivity or presuppositions, and if the translators are free to alter the objective biblical text with the notion that they are making it more readable, relevant or less offensive (this is especially true in paraphrases such as *The Message*), then why can't a local church or Christian leaders do the same in their teaching? If the sense of a passage of Scripture is up for grabs, if your understanding is as good as mine, and if a text has more than one meaning and all meanings are equally justified, then why study the Bible at all? Why not think up something you want to teach and then run to the Scriptures to try to find a passage that supports your views?

Of course, this has been an all too common practice for years. But now there is a new twist. When a leader wants to develop a certain thesis and ground it in the Scriptures, but no objectively understood passage can support this particular notion, what is to be done? He might force a passage out of context and simply misinterpret it, hoping no one notices. Or he might allegorize or spiritualize the passage, adding a foreign meaning. But all of this has been done before. A novel approach, one that might work even better, is to get creative and find a translation or paraphrase that will back his claim — even if that translation has seriously distorted the passage. With this final methodology there is the advantage of actually using the Scriptures as the authority and a fair amount of certainty that few will ever bother to check the passage for its accuracy and context. All of this brings to mind Peter's comments concerning the untaught and unstable distorting the Scriptures to their own destruction (2 Peter 3:16). The word 'distort' in that verse basically means 'to torture'. It is the idea of twisting Scripture to make it mean something it was not intended to mean, with the end result being our own destruction.

This last accusation seems mean-spirited at best, but the evidence is rapidly coming in that such is the latest rage. I first discovered this new fad when I visited some market-driven evangelical churches. Here were churches that, to my knowledge, still preach the gospel and hold to most of the fundamentals of the faith. Their worship services were crowded and full of enthusiasm. Spiritual life appeared to flow as the congregations sang praise choruses. But something was missing — Bibles. In one church of over 400 I saw only a handful of people carrying Bibles. I wondered why until I sat through the service and found that Bibles were not needed. The Scriptures were never opened, never read. When the pastor preached at least he did open his Bible, but he asked no one to open theirs, nor did he expect anyone to do so. He preached a message loosely based on Scripture and throughout his sermon his main points were projected on the overhead screens along with a few Scripture verses. While the superficiality of the message and the lack of Bibles disturbed me, at least, I thought, he did preach from the Bible and at least verses were projected on the screens. But still, a church with no open Bibles created the scent of spiritual death to me. Was I just being too picky? Many who come to church today are biblically illiterate. They can barely find Genesis, let alone Ezekiel.

With a little research and input from others I began to realize that what I had experienced was not an unusual event. Churches all across the land are following the same methodologies. Apparently the church-growth leaders have been recommending this approach and their disciples have jumped on board — in many cases, perhaps, without serious evaluation. But it is dangerous for Christians to close their Bibles. What are Bereans to do without their Bibles? What if the leadership of the church has an agenda they want to foster and they misuse the Scriptures to promote it? Who would examine the Word and 'see whether these things are so' (Acts 17:11). It appeared to me to be a dangerous trend.

The Purpose-Driven Life

About that time I picked up Rick Warren's runaway bestseller, *The Purpose-Driven Life*. Warren's book promises to be 'a guide to a 40-day spiritual journey that will enable you to discover the answers to life's most important question: What on earth am I here for?' More than that, 'By the end of this journey you will know God's purpose for your life and will understand the big picture — how all the pieces of your life fit together' (p.9). With this kind of promo and with Warren's notoriety, we would expect his book to sell well, and it has. Not only is it the number one best selling Christian book at the time of this writing but thousands of churches have jumped on board his 40-day spiritual journey.

First, we should say a word or two about Warren himself and his book in general. His first book, *The Purpose-Driven Church,* has greatly influenced churches throughout the world, due certainly to the fact that the church he pastors, Saddleback Church in southern California, is one of the largest churches in America, and a trendsetter among new paradigm churches. Saddleback reports that over 300,000 pastors from over 100 countries have been trained at their leadership conferences. Warren obviously has astounding influence over churches throughout the world.

There are a number of similarities between *The Purpose-Driven Church* and *The Purpose-Driven Life*. Both, for instance, offer some good sound advice, helpful biblical insight and practical suggestions — and both are riddled with errors throughout. The highly discerning reader can perhaps sift through the wheat and tares and make a good loaf of bread, but most readers, I fear, will swallow the poison along with the substance. This leads me to ask, 'Who is Warren's audience?' I was thoroughly bewildered as to whom the author was trying to connect. If it is a book for the unsaved then he fails, for the gospel is never clearly presented. The closest he came was when he wrote, 'Real life begins by committing yourself completely to Jesus Christ' (p. 58). In Warren's gospel presentations no mention is made of sin, repentance or even the Cross. Real life (i.e., a life with purpose) seems to be the reward, and lack of real life (purpose) the problem. The thesis of *The Purpose-Driven Life* is stated, I believe, on page twenty-five: 'We discover that meaning and purpose only when we make God the reference point of our lives.'

Warren's message is this: find God and you will find yourself (purpose). We will agree that meaning and purpose will be a reality to the Christian, but they are not the objects of the gospel itself. The gospel is that we as rebellious sinners have offended a holy God, are dead in our sins, are enslaved to sin and the devil, and are under the wrath of God. But God, rich in mercy, sent his Son to die as our substitute to redeem us from our lost condition and give us eternal life. We receive this gift by faith as we turn to Christ, and from sin (Eph. 2:1-10). That our life takes on new purpose at that point is absolutely true. However, we do not come to Christ because we sense a lack of purpose, but because God has opened our eyes to our need for forgiveness of sin and a relationship with him. This is one of the fatal flaws in the market-driven church's message in which the unbeliever is called to follow Christ in order to receive any number of benefits — fulfilment, self-esteem, improved marriage, a thrilling lifestyle, or purpose, rather than freedom from sin, the righteousness of God and the gift of eternal salvation. We must never confuse the benefits of the gospel with the gospel itself.

If Warren is writing for new believers, which seems the case due to the elementary tone and substance of the whole book, he again misses the mark, for he uses many expressions and biblical references that would be unfamiliar to the novice. On the other hand, if he is writing to the mature he has wasted paper, for any semi-well-taught believer will be completely bored with this book. So, while much praise will surely be lavished on *The Purpose-Driven Life*, it escapes me who will really profit.

Be that as it may, I want to give credit where credit is due. Warren writes some good sections on a number of subjects, including worship, community, the church, truth and spiritual gifts. If some of these topics could be isolated from the main body, they would make for helpful reading. But when interspersed with an array of erroneous ideas, distortions of Scripture and plain false teaching, they are of little value and may prove dangerous.

As I began reading this book, the problems were so numerous and obvious that I backed up and began marking these errors. I found forty-two biblical inaccuracies, eighteen out-of-context passages of Scripture, supposedly used to prove his point, and another nine distorted translations. (I will return to some of these in a moment.)

In general, there is much that is disturbing within the pages of *The Purpose-Driven Life*. Even though he denies it, Warren is obviously a disciple of pop-psychology, which is littered throughout. The wise reader is well aware that simply because someone denies he is teaching something does not mean he is not teaching it. The proof is not in the denial but in the substance. In this case Warren on the one hand repeatedly rejects psycho-babble, but on the other hand he immerses his reader in it. One example is 'Most conflict is rooted in unmet needs' (p.154). You will find this idea in Rogers and Freud but try to find it in Scripture. He quoted favourably from a wide variety of dubious authors, from Aldous Huxley and Albert Schweitzer to George Bernard Shaw and St. John of the Cross (Catholic mystic). He apparently believes practising Roman Catholics are true believers, several times mentioning monks and nuns as Christian examples, and there is of course the obligatory reference to Mother Teresa (twice). This unqualified acceptance and promotion of Catholics brings into question Warren's understanding of the gospel message itself. If he believes that faithful Roman Catholics, who believe in a works-righteousness, are born-again Christians, what does he believe the gospel is? Do we receive the gift of salvation by faith alone, or by faith plus certain works and sacraments? This is no minor issue, especially in a book that never spells out the plan of salvation.

Warren, however, is not totally off base, and I would not want to portray him as such. Without question he is as evangelical as many evangelicals. Nevertheless, when every third page (on average) of a book presents either an unbiblical, or at least a biblically unsupportable idea, there is not much sense bothering to read it. And that would be my suggestion — don't bother.

Torturing Scripture

What we want to do in the remainder of our examination of Warren's popular book is to point out some examples of his distortion of Scripture. This is not to say that everything he says is wrong. The irony is that often he will say something that is biblically correct, but rather than use proper scriptural support he chooses to force the meaning of another passage to prove his point. Our concern here is focused on his blatant twisting of the biblical text to suit his purposes. This is a dangerous trend that will lead to nothing good if not recognized, challenged and rejected by the Christian community.

Matthew 16:25

As stated above, it is not unusual for Warren to make good statements, such as his rejection of pop-psychology, and then turn around and by his misuse of Scripture promote the very thing he just condemned. The reader is then faced with two problems: what does Warren really believe about this subject and, more importantly, why has he chosen to distort the Word of God either directly or through his use of faulty translations? For example, in the midst of his denial of pop-psychology (p.19) he quotes *The Message* translation of Matthew 16:25 — 'Self-help is no help at all. Self-sacrifice is the way, my way, *to finding yourself*, your true self' (emphasis mine). *The Message* has altered the meaning of Jesus' words into a means by which a person finds himself, a fad having roots back to the 1960s but not to the Bible. Compare the NASB rendering: 'For whoever wishes to save his life shall lose it; but whoever loses his life for My sake shall find it.' Jesus is speaking of eternal life (v. 26 makes this clear), not the modern day concept of 'finding yourself'. There is a bit of bait-and-switch going on in many of these quotations. Warren is attempting to tap into the current felt needs — in this case finding ourselves or our purpose in life. He is then presenting the Christian life as a means of meeting that felt need. It is true that the Lord will give you purpose in life, but that purpose will be to live for and follow Christ. It is not a promise that we will find ourselves (if you ever find yourself you are going to be disappointed anyway) but that we will find true life in Christ. What often happens is subtle: Warren turns these passages, and the Christian life, from being Christ-centred to being centred on the human self, the individual. We now become the focus rather than Christ.

Romans 12:3

The thesis of the book is found on page 25, where Warren says, 'We discover that meaning and purpose only when we make God the reference point of our lives.' He then quotes from *The Message* paraphrase of Romans 12:3, 'The *only accurate way to understand ourselves* is by what God is and by what he does for us' (emphasis mine). *The Message* has subtly changed the meaning of the text. To see how, we turn to a good translation. The NASB reads, 'For by the grace given to me I say to every man among you not to think more highly of himself than he ought to think; but to think so as to have sound judgment, as God has allotted to each a measure of faith.' The thrust of the verse is the problem of pride, in the context of spiritual gifts (see vv. 4-8). Apparently, some in the church body were arrogant about their spiritual gifts, leading to anger, bitterness and vengeance (see vv. 9-21). Paul told them not to think so highly of themselves but to have sound judgment in reference to their giftedness. The result would be the proper functioning of the body. The passage is not giving a formula for how to understand ourselves. *The Message* abuses the true meaning of the text and yet Warren quotes it to support his thesis.

In both of these examples, Warren's use of Scripture is just close enough to be confusing, but neither of these passages is being used as it was meant to be. This is not a minor issue. Once we believe we have the right to change the meaning of God's Word to suit our agenda, there is no limit as to how far the misrepresentation of God's truth can go. This is exactly how virtually every cult and heresy is started. While I am not accusing Warren of this level of deception, it should greatly concern us to see him adopting the same attitude toward the Scriptures. And it should disturb us even more to discover that so few Christians care.

I Corinthians 2:7

In chapter one, Warren makes several statements with which I would agree. He writes that the Bible 'explains what no self-help or philosophy book could know' (p.20). He then quotes 1 Corinthians 2:7 from *The Message* paraphrase as support: 'God's wisdom … goes deep into the interior of his purposes … It's not the latest message, but more like the oldest — what God determined as the *way to bring out his best in us*' (emphasis mine). Let's first compare this to a good translation. The NASB reads, 'But we speak God's wisdom in a mystery, the hidden wisdom, which God predestined before the ages to our glory.' Just a quick reading reveals that *The Message's* paraphrase has no real connection with the meaning Paul was intending. Paul was writing of the wisdom of God, which is unlike the world's wisdom in several ways. First, it is a mystery, which in Scripture speaks of something hidden in the past and unknowable without revelation from God (see Eph. 3:3-5). God's wisdom is still hidden from the people of the world (vv. 6, 8), but revealed to God's people through the Holy Spirit in the New Testament Scriptures. God had determined this wisdom before time began but has now worked it out in the present age. All of this was for '*our glory*'. In the context of the passage this refers to the eternal salvation of God's people as a result of the crucifixion of Christ (see v. 8). '*Our glory*' is biblical language referring to the final goal of salvation which is to share in the glory of the Lord himself (v. 8b). Now, let's back up to Warren and his use of *The Message*. The wisdom of God that has been revealed through the apostle Paul is not that God has determined 'the way to bring out His best in us', but that the Lord has determined the way to bring us to eternal glory. It is not about purpose in life, but about the truth of salvation. It is not that Warren's original statement is wrong. He could have actually found passages of Scripture to support his view. The problem is that he is misusing Scripture, in rather imaginative fashion, to prove his position. Once we head down this slippery slope it will prove very difficult to change courses.

Ephesians 1:11

A similar type of thing happens in the very next paragraph of the book. Warren makes a biblically defensible statement: 'You must build your life on eternal truths, not pop psychology, success-motivation, or inspirational stories.' Excellent! But rather than backing this truth with proper Scripture, he decides to use a distorted paraphrase of Ephesians 1:11 found in *The Message* once again. It reads, 'It's in Christ that we *find out who we are and what we are living for.* Long before we first heard of Christ and got our hopes up, he had his *eyes on us, had designs on us for glorious living*, part of the overall purpose he is working out in everything and everyone' (emphasis mine). Warren says that this quote gives us three insights into our purpose, the first of which is, 'You discover your identity and purpose through a relationship with Jesus Christ.'
In analyzing these comments we begin with a literal translation of the verse: 'Also we have obtained an inheritance, having been predestined according to His purpose who works all things after the counsel of His will' (NASB). This verse says nothing about *discovering* our purpose through a relationship with Christ. It speaks about our position in Christ — our eternal inheritance in him. This verse tells us that we have been made the heirs of God; through no merit of our own we were given the right to all the blessings of salvation, both now and in eternity. It speaks of being 'predestined according to His purpose', not finding our purpose or identity.

Jeremiah 29:11

A more common form of misuse of Scripture is taking passages out of context. Warren gives this exaggerated promise: 'If you have felt hopeless, hold on! Wonderful changes are going to happen in your life as you begin to live it on purpose', followed up with this quote from Jeremiah 29:11: 'I know what I am planning for you

... I have good plans for you, not plans to hurt you. I will give you hope and a good future' (p.31). Unfortunately, this is a promise to Israel concerning their future, not a general promise for all people (even Christians) at all times. Just a few chapters later the promise is reversed: 'Behold, I am watching over them for harm and not for good...' (44:27). In Lamentations 3:38 the same prophet writes, 'Is it not from the mouth of the Most High that both good and ill go forth?' It is strange how people love to claim Jeremiah 29:11 and ignore passages such as these last two. I have yet to find anyone who has claimed Jeremiah 44:27 as their life's verse.

Genesis 6:8

Chapter nine is devoted to the kind of person who makes God smile and is rooted in this *Living Bible* paraphrase of Genesis 6:8: 'Noah was a pleasure to the Lord.' The *New King James* translates this verse: 'Noah found grace in the eyes of the Lord.' Some other literal versions translate 'grace' as 'favour' and the Hebrew word can have that meaning. But when used of God, the word always means unmerited favour or grace. When Noah found grace, he was the recipient of undeserved Divine favour. He was not spared the flood because of his righteousness, but because of God's grace. By changing the word from 'grace' to 'pleasure', the *Living Bible* has turned the true meaning of the passage on its head. Now Noah is spared due to his goodness — he is the kind of guy that makes God smile — and you can be such a person too. But now grace is no longer grace; it has been transformed into a work that pleases God. This is not a minor error; it strikes at the root of the Christian faith. Ironically, Genesis 6:9, which tells us that 'Noah was a righteous man, blameless in his time, and Noah walked with God', could have been used to support Warren's chapter, so keep in mind our concern. We are not accusing Warren of being wrong in everything he is saying, but we are accusing him of distorting Scripture. He is undermining the Word of God by changing its meaning to suit his purposes. In this case the marvellous doctrine of grace takes the hit.

Job 22:21

Warren strains Scripture to interesting limits by using none other than Eliphaz as his spokesman. 'The Bible is crystal clear about how you benefit when you fully surrender your life to God. First you experience peace' (p.82). The proof-text is Job 22:21: 'Stop quarreling with God! If you agree with him, you will have peace at last, and things will go well for you.' If you recall, this speech from Job's friend is a promotion of works-righteousness which, along with Eliphaz's whole theology of living, will be condemned by God later in the book. To use it as a means of finding peace with God is an extremely careless use of Scripture.

Romans 6:17

In the same paragraph Warren also promises freedom if we surrender to God. He uses *The Message*'s rendering of Romans 6:17: 'Offer yourselves to the ways of God and the freedom never quits … [his] commands set you free to live openly in freedom!' It is true that we have been set free in Christ, but what kind of freedom is Paul offering? The NASB translates this verse: 'But thanks be to God that though you were slaves of sin, you became obedient from the heart to that form of teaching to which you were committed.' Verse eighteen continues, 'And having been freed from sin, you became slaves of righteousness.' Warren does not mention that the freedom promised in Scripture is from sin, and that the believer becomes immediately the slave of another — righteousness. Nor is there any mention that this slavery transferral is *not* predicated upon a subsequent surrender on the part of the Christian, but is rather the definition of a Christian. When people come to Christ for salvation, their master is changed. They no longer owe any allegiance to sin for they have become the slave of God. Whether they live in fidelity to this new Master is another matter, but ownership has changed hands. This is the argument of Romans 6, which is ignored by Warren, who forces it to say what God never intended.

Hebrews 12:1

Warren uses *The Living Bible* paraphrase of Hebrews 12:1 to teach that God has assigned certain boundaries to each believer. 'When we try to overextend our ministry reach beyond what God shaped us for, we experience stress. Just as each runner in a race is given a different lane to run in, we must individually "run with patience the particular race that God has set before us"' (p.253). But this verse simply reads, 'Let us run with endurance the race that is set before us' (NASB), and is speaking of the Christian race of faith in general. This verse cannot be pressed to teach that each Christian has a *particular* race to run — it is simply not the context or meaning of the passage.

Philippians 4:7

We are told that 'Worry is the warning light that God has been shoved to the sideline. The moment you put him back at the center, you will have peace again' (p.314). He then quotes *The Message's* translation of Philippians 4:7: 'A sense of God's wholeness … will come and settle you down. It's wonderful what happens when Christ displaces worry at the center of your life.' While there may be truth in what Warren says, a proper translation of this verse will not teach what he says it does: 'And the peace of God which surpasses all comprehension, shall guard your hearts and minds in Christ Jesus' (NASB). Let's break it down a bit. 'A sense of God's wholeness', whatever that means, is not the same thing as the peace of God. The last sentence found in *The Message* is foreign to the passage. The peace of God guarding our hearts and minds cannot be contorted to mean that something wonderful happens when Christ displaces worry at the centre of your life. Warren is developing his propositions upon faulty paraphrases of Scripture and the average reader is none the wiser. Placing God back at the centre of your life may indeed result in peace, but Philippians 4:7 does not say so. To make Scripture say what it does not say is manipulation, not exegesis.

Of course we could go on, but hopefully you get the point. Other notable examples are:

Page 24 – James 1:18
Pages 25, 30 – Isaiah 49:4
Page 104 – 1 Corinthians 14:16-17
Page 105 – Romans 12:1, 2
Page 109 – Job 23: 8-10
Page 110 – Job 7:11
Page 219 – 2 Corinthians 3:18
Page 223 – Habakkuk 2:3
Page 232 – Mark 8:35
Pages 272-273 – 1 Corinthians 1:27
Pages 273 – 2 Corinthians 12:9-10

Summary

So, what difference does it make? What if Warren is misrepresenting Scripture over forty times as well as peppering his book with extra-biblical psychological theories and other earthly pieces of wisdom, disguised as biblical principles? Overall he says many good things, and even in the sections where Scripture is abused he often says the right thing but uses wrong Scripture to support it. What's the big deal? The big deal is this: once we sign off on this kind of Christian teaching and torturing of Scripture, the sky is the limit. It should not go without notice that every cult claims to believe in the Bible. The uniqueness of cults is that they twist the interpretation of Scripture to say what they want it to say, and failing that they write their own translations to support their heresies (e.g. Jehovah Witnesses' *New World Bible*). Should we endorse these same methodologies when evangelicals promote them? Or should we refute those who openly sanction such approaches to Scripture? Remember we are not discussing different opinions on interpretations of certain passages. That too cannot be ignored. But of a more serious nature is this careless and wanton mishandling of Scripture that we have been discussing. To purposely ignore the proper translation of a passage and insert one that has no basis in the original languages in order to undergird a particular point of view is about the most dangerous thing that I can imagine. The only thing more concerning would be to discover large segments of the evangelical community being incapable of discerning this kind of problem — and not caring.

11

The Authority and Sufficiency of Scripture

Perhaps the most important issue facing the church today is the matter of authority. Who or what has the right, the authority, to determine what we believe and how we are to live? The answer to that question, not so very long ago, was quite uncomplicated — at least to evangelical Christians. The Word of God was the final authority over all areas of faith and practice. One of the battle cries of the Reformation was *sola Scriptura* — Scripture alone. This simply meant that the ultimate basis of authority and truth was Scripture. Scripture had the final say over all we believed and how we lived those beliefs. More than that, the Bible was seen as sufficient. That is, what the Word had to say was adequate to equip us for every good work (2 Tim. 3:17). No one claimed that Scripture exhausted every subject — or even addressed some (e.g., mathematics). But where it did not give direct teaching it gave principles by which we could examine and evaluate all things 'pertaining to life and godliness' (2 Peter 1:3). That Scripture claims for itself such authority and sufficiency was widely accepted based upon numerous passages (e.g., John 17:17; Mark 12:24; Luke 11:25; 16:27-31; Heb. 4:12; James 1:25; 1 Peter 2:2; Acts 20:20-32; Ps. 19, 119; 2 Tim. 3:15-17; 2 Peter 1:3; Matt. 5:17-20; 12:18-27; 26:52-54; Luke 10:25-26; 16:17). But, for the most part, the evangelical church today does not believe this. The authority and sufficiency of God's Word is being supplanted at every turn.

However, before we observe the modern church, let's back up and look at the recent past. What is transpiring today has a familiar ring to it. This has all happened before — and not that long ago.

Epistemology

The issue of authority largely deals with epistemology, that is, how we discover and determine truth. Without racing down philosophical rabbit trails of which there are many, the answer is that our knowledge of truth must come from a source. When reduced to 'basic' possibilities the sources of truth are limited to three:

Humans

If one believes that humans are the final source of truth we are still left with the epistemological question of how we discover this truth. James Draper and Kenneth Keathley give this helpful overview:

> The person holding to human reason (or rationalism) believes he is his own final authority. The question then is which method that individual will use in testing truth claims. The options available to him can be grouped under three headings: rationalism, empiricism, and mysticism. The rationalist believes he or she can determine what is true by reason alone, because of innate or natural abilities within the human mind. The empiricist places confidence in experimentation and in the observation of sense phenomena, affirming as true only that which can be physically demonstrated. Finally, there is the mystic, who rejects rationalism and empiricism because he recognizes that the individual is not capable of arriving at ultimate truth either by reason or observation. The mystic, however, believes that the individual does possess extrarational abilities that enable him to intuit truth. Truth, the mystic contends, cannot be known objectively; it can be encountered only subjectively. No matter which of the three approaches are employed by human reason, they all have this in common: They make the individual the final arbiter of truth.[1]

Religion

Within the Christian tradition this is best represented by the Roman Church. According to Catholic theology, it is the Church that has given us the Bible and, therefore, has final authority. The Roman Church would technically not claim to hold views contrary to Scripture, but it is the Church which interprets Scripture and is free to add to it. Therefore, any apparent contradiction, for example praying to Mary or the saints, is resolved by Rome's claim to authority.

Revelation

If God exists, it is not difficult to believe that He has communicated to mankind. The Bible claims to be that revelation. Conservative Christians throughout the ages, and especially since the Reformation, have recognized the exclusive claim of Scripture to be the complete and final Word of God for this age. This is not to say that there have not been many usurpers to this claim.

Yesterday and today

One of the great challenges faced by Christians in the not too distant past drew from a number of sources: German rationalism, higher criticism, enlightenment thought, etc., ultimately evolving into what we call Christian liberalism today. The father of liberalism is usually recognized as Friedrich Schleiermacher (1768-1834), professor of theology at the University of Berlin. Joining many popular philosophical systems with Christianity, Schleiermacher came to distrust any form of authority. But he did not want to reject Christianity, recognizing that mankind needs religion. He reasoned that propositional revelation about God may be faulty or even nonexistent but, since man needs religious experience, the outer shell of Christianity must be retained. The Bible may be untrustworthy, shot through with error, unreliable for developing a living framework, but it is still possible to experience God through religious expressions. The foundation may be gone, but somehow the walls are still standing. Such people are convinced that they encounter God as they connect with the 'divine spark' found in every human, or through mystical practices, or through subjective experiences. They are unconcerned with the authority of Scripture — to them the Bible is riddled with errors, but that does not matter as long as they can have an existential relationship with God — or at least, so they think. William James, certainly no evangelical Christian, made an astute observation over one hundred years ago about the encroachment of liberal thought within Christianity:

> The advance of liberalism, so-called, in Christianity, during the past fifty years, may fairly be called a victory of healthy-mindedness within the church over the morbidness with which the old hell-fire theology was more harmoniously related. We have now whole congregations whose preachers, far from magnifying our consciousness of sin, seem devoted rather to making little of it. They ignore, or even deny, eternal punishment, and insist on the dignity rather than on the depravity of man. They look at the continual preoccupation of the old-fashioned Christian with the salvation of his soul as something sickly and reprehensible rather than admirable; and a sanguine and 'muscular' attitude, which to our forefathers would have seemed purely heathen, has become in their eyes an ideal element of Christian character. I am not asking whether or not they are right, I am only pointing out the change.[2]

James' assessment has a modern ring to it. Old liberalism has been waning in the last few decades, but certainly has not gone away. Rather, it has combined with other errant theological threads and morphed into a number of forms. Take for example the recent comments syndicated columnist and liberal Episcopal priest, Tom Ehrich, wrote:

> Picture a prosperous suburban congregation, set among big houses and private schools, populated by professionals and young families, once known for its intellectual vitality, now caught up in stick-to-the-Bible orthodoxy ... Preaching there, says a member, rarely strays from a

word-by-word explication of assigned texts. Adult education classes tend to be 'led by people who regard the Bible as "inerrant" and allow no questioning. We never hear an open, honest exploration of what it means to live as a Christian in today's world' ... Clearly, some sort of retreat is under way. Like all retreats, it claims the moral high ground. But what I see in the 'land of the free and home of the brave' is dogmatic conformity (fear of freedom) and intolerance (fear of the other) ... What concerns me is the emergence of a religious leadership cadre who don't hesitate to turn fearfulness into rage, hatred and scapegoating. They, of all people, should know better. They should know that the answer to fear is faith, not hatred. **They should know that Jesus didn't name enemies, launch moral crusades or wage culture wars. He didn't exercise thought-control with his disciples. He didn't insist on one way of thinking or believing, He wasn't legalistic or rigid or conformist** (emphasis mine).[3]

This sounds like the rantings of old-fashioned liberalism — but wait! Many within evangelicalism are echoing the same tune. Taking a stand for the truth is long since out of vogue. John MacArthur makes the point: 'It is no longer deemed necessary to fight for the truth. In fact, many evangelicals now consider it ill-mannered and uncharitable to argue about any point of doctrine.'[4]

Liberalism has joined forces with postmodernism to challenge the teachings of the Bible. Meanwhile, many in evangelicalism are sitting on the sidelines wanting to be tolerant and attempting to bully and intimidate any who advocate discernment. It is little wonder then that a new wave of liberalism is sweeping over Christianity. The seeker-sensitive church has been seen by many as just old liberalism in disguise, but that is not altogether true. The seeker-sensitive church has fudged on many biblical truths,[5] but it still embraces most of the cardinal doctrines and still seeks to proclaim the gospel, even if its message is often out of balance with the New Testament. But the seeker-sensitive church has given birth to a new movement being called the emergent church. The emergent church is taking to logical conclusion what the seeker-sensitive church began. All dressed up in post-modern religious garb the emergent church is rapidly rejecting and undermining almost all biblical theology. In other words the emergent church is the new liberalism. Evangelicalism is reaping what it has sown (for more on the emerging church see chapters 14 and 15).

But what about all of the spiritual interest that is evident. Christian books and music top the charts. Megachurches are bursting at the seams. Some are proclaiming that we may be in the midst of the greatest revival since Pentecost. In response, I agree with a Gallup poll evaluation from a few years ago. 'We are having a revival of feelings, but not of the knowledge of God. The church today is more guided by feeling than by convictions. We value enthusiasm more than informed commitment.'[6]

If this is true why are so few noticing it? Let me make a few suggestions:

1. Because the marketers of this approach to Christianity have become adept at giving people what they want. Michael Horton writes, 'Throughout the prophetic literature, we notice a common theme — the false prophets tell the people what they want to hear, baptize it with God's name, and serve it up as God's latest word to His people.'[7]

2. Because the centrality of the Word of God has been subtly replaced with inferior but pleasing substitutes. Systematic preaching and teaching of the Bible has been displaced in many churches with entertainment, drama, concerts, comic acts, and the like. For a number of decades psychological theory has been usurping the authority of Scripture. The purpose of many churches is no longer salvation and sanctification, but therapy. And, increasingly, mysticism and extra-biblical revelations are superseding the Bible.

3. Because so many within evangelicalism are drifting with the tide of worldly thought and opinion. Pascal said, 'When everything is moving at once, nothing appears

to be moving, as on board ship. When everyone is moving towards depravity, no one seems to be moving, but if someone stops, he shows up the others who are rushing on by acting as a fixed point.'[8] Commenting on this statement Douglas Groothuis wrote, 'The fixed point in a shifting world is biblical truth and all that agrees with it.'[9] Preceding Pascal's quote, Groothuis had this to say: 'We are told that Christians must shift their emphasis from objective truth to communal experience, from rational argument to subjective appeal, from doctrinal orthodoxy to relevant practices. I have reasoned ... that this move is nothing less than fatal to Christian integrity and biblical witness. It is also illogical philosophically. We have something far better to offer.'[10]

Peter informs us: 'His divine power has granted to us everything pertaining to life and godliness' (2 Peter 1:3a). How is this life and godliness found? 'Through the true knowledge of Him who called us by His own glory and excellence' (1:3b). And where is the knowledge of Christ found? In the precious Word of God. No wonder Peter encouraged us to be 'like newborn babes, [who] long for the pure milk of the Word, that by it you may grow in respect to salvation' (1 Peter 2:2). Why feed at the trough of worldly wisdom or mystical experience when we have the final, complete, infallible revelation from God that is able to 'make us wise unto salvation' (2 Tim. 3:15), 'and equip us for every good work' (2 Tim. 3:17)? I agree with Groothuis, we Bible-believing Christians do have something better to offer.

Pressing Challenges

12

The Challenge of Mysticism: Part I

I am often asked what I see as the next important challenge facing evangelical Christianity. Such questions are asked in the wake of major movements that have changed the face of evangelicalism in the last two decades, including the market-driven church and the closely related 'Purpose Driven Life' (PDL) campaigns that have so greatly impacted God's people. The legacy of both of these movements will not be that the church discovered new ways of worship, or new methodologies to replace the outdated. Instead, I fear that they will be remembered by future generations for their undermining of the authority of Scripture. To be sure these movements were not the genesis of the lack of confidence in God's Word — there have been many forerunners. Actually they have capitalized upon this trend and have taken it to a new level. It is not that everything the church growth experts and PDL espouses is wrong; it is that the authority for what the church now believes has shifted. It has shifted from the infallible Scriptures to psychological and sociological experts, opinions of the masses, trends of the moment and the philosophy of pragmatism. This shift has been subtle, which has made it all the more dangerous.

Few have bothered to deny the Bible itself, they just misquote it, abuse its meaning, force their opinion on it, and if necessary mistranslate it to give the appearance that the Scriptures are backing their claims. The effect of all of this scriptural manipulation is to erode both the authority of God's Word and to give the appearance what Scripture has to say isn't really important. It is only a short step from here to a Christian community that no longer has much use for the Bible. As a matter of fact, if the increased popularity of people coming to church services without their Bibles, sermons being reduced to PowerPoint presentations and sermon note taking digressed to fill-in-the-blank outlines, are any indication, we may be there now.

Such Christianity is devoid of the majesty of God and the wonder of his Word. It is only a matter of time until true believers grow tired of this insipid brand of evangelicalism with its 7-11 choruses (seven words sung eleven times); its dramatizations; its dumbed-down Bible teaching; its latest fad that promises to change lives but does not; and its 'me-centred' orientation. When (and as) they do, they will turn in a number of directions. Happily, some will come back to the Word and to churches that faithfully proclaim it. Some will head to Roman Catholicism and Orthodox for more liturgical, traditional and authoritative expressions. Still others will write off the faith and declare that 'it doesn't work for me'.

As we might expect, we are seeing these things now, and will increasingly in the future. But many thirsty believers, wanting something more, something deeper than has been their experience, are also becoming infatuated with two other overlapping fads. One of these is ancient, harkening back to premodern times (mysticism). The other is new and considers itself postmodern (the emerging church). They both have in common disdain for modernity, a distortion of Scripture and a rejection of much that conservative Christians hold dear. Despite these flaws both are rapidly gaining popularity, especially among the young, which seems to be the targeted demographic.

Let me be very clear about what I am trying to communicate: There is only a superficial, yet growing, link between the market-driven church (including PDL) movement and mysticism and the emerging church movements. And while the market-driven church is not a direct conduit to mysticism and postmodernism, it certainly has opened the door. By hollowing out the core of biblical substance and replacing it with superficial theological fluff, the movement has created a hunger for true spirituality. One can only live so long on cotton candy before a steak, or at least a hamburger, is craved. As more and more Christians tire of their spiritual diet many are turning to even more unhealthy alternatives. It is these alternatives that we are describing.

The trend which I will address first is the one embracing mysticism which has its roots in medieval Roman Catholic monks and hermits (the Desert Fathers). This mysticism promises to bring us into contact with God in ways not experienced by most believers, and is especially appealing to those tired of watered down Christianity.

The other leaning is toward postmodernity. Many, including myself, have referred to the market-driven church as postmodern, and while they have some characteristics of this worldview, they would not consider themselves to be postmodern by the normal understanding of the term. As a matter of fact they would strongly deny that they were postmodern and would give evidence of their similar doctrinal beliefs to historical evangelicalism. But a truly postmodern 'evangelical' movement has arisen, which boldly affirms its postmodern understanding of life in general and Christianity in particular. This movement, which for now calls itself the 'emerging church', is extremely popular on college campuses and among twenty-somethings, although many of its leaders are middle-aged. But before we tackle the emerging church we need to spend considerable time dealing with mysticism. Our starting point will be to grasp the meaning of mysticism in a Christian context, and then examine how it was practiced in ancient times. This will help us get a handle on why it is becoming all the rage today.

Mysticism defined

The first obstacle encountered when discussing mysticism is trying to define it. When I once declared in print that Henry Blackaby is a Christian mystic, a young man wrote his master's thesis challenging my claim, proving that Blackaby was more in line with pietism than classical mysticism. His point was well taken when using, as he was, a formal definition of a mystic. I was using the term more loosely as represented by this quote from John MacArthur,

> The mystic disdains rational understanding and seeks truth instead through the feelings, the imagination, personal visions, inner voices, private illumination, or other purely subjective means.[1]

By this rather loose definition Blackaby is indeed a mystic. This type of mysticism, which I believe to be a functional denial of *sola scriptura,* is running rampant throughout the Christian community with devastating consequences. But in the more technical, official sense MacArthur's definition is inadequate. Classical mysticism, which is now making a strong return to Christianity, goes far deeper. Someone has said mysticism 'begins with a mist and always ends in schism', and that is not far from the truth. Mysticism is the search for *unio mystica*, personal union with God.[2] But what does this union encompass and how is it attained?

Here things get sticky, for as Georgia Harkness tells us in her book, *Mysticism*, there are at least twenty-six definitions of mysticism by those who have studied it carefully.[3] Winfried Corduan, in his *Mysticism: an Evangelical Option?* boils it down to the essentials when he writes, 'The mystic believes that there is an absolute and that he or she can enjoy an **unmediated link** to this absolute in a superrational experience' (emphasis mine).[4] But even here there are at least three distinct categories of mysticism: panenthenic, in which, as Carl Jung thought, a segment of the collective unconscious intrudes on the conscious mind; monistic such as found in Hinduism and Buddhism whereby the individual is merged into the impersonal All, whatever that is called; and theistic in which the absolute is God, although not necessarily the true God.[5] The actual experience by these various types of mystics is very similar. But with whom the mystic believes they come into union is determined by the mystic's belief system, as William James' research demonstrated decades ago.[6]

The road to mysticism

The journey to mystical experience, almost universally, involves three stages: purgation, illumination and union.

Purgation

Purgation is the cleansing stage which begins with self-examination and penitence and leads to a holy life. Sixteenth-century monk, St. John of the Cross, is best known for his description of this stage which he called the 'dark night of the soul'. During the dark night of the soul an individual feels abandoned by God, spiritually dry and at the point of despair. John saw this as a way in which God purified the soul through suffering, for only when the soul has been purified is it in a position to experience a rapturous union with God. This purgation involved detachment from the things of the world including material and physical desires, and mortification, the building of new paths to replace the old ones now rejected.

Illumination

At some point the purgation stage bleeds over into the illumination stage in which the mystic begins to experience inner voices and visions. The goal of illumination is to know genuine spiritual truth, but such truth cannot be found in conventional or even rational ways. This differs, at least in theory from the 'mystical' Christian as defined earlier by MacArthur. These still believe that truth is primarily found through rational means, but they feel their thoughts and mental impressions can be explained as the inner voice of God. The true mystic has come to the conclusion that the secret and 'deep' things of God cannot be understood rationally. They can only be understood through the experience of illumination.

One of the earliest Christian mystics, known as Pseudo-Dionysius, taught that to achieve the ultimate prize of union with God, 'The soul must lose the inhibitions of the senses and of reason. God is beyond the intellect, beyond goodness itself, and it is through unknowing, and the discarding of human concepts, that the soul returns to God and is united with the "ray of divine darkness."'[7] The means by which mystics achieved illumination was through fasting, long seasons of specialized prayers known as contemplative prayers and by following various spiritual disciplines of which the best known today were designed by the Catholic monk and founder of the Jesuits, Ignatius Loyola. As we will see later, it is upon Ignatius' *Spiritual Exercises* that Richard Foster patterns his famous book, *The Celebration of Discipline.*

Union

The ultimate goal of the mystic is unmediated union with God. This point, at which the soul attains oneness with God, 'was the mystical ecstasy in which, for a brief indescribable moment, all barriers seemed to be swept away and new insight supernaturally imparted as one gave himself over fully to the Infinite One'.[8] The ancient mystics would frame this experience in romantic, even sensual terms. John of the Cross 'describes the union in terms of spiritual betrothal, where the soul, conceived of as feminine, is married to Christ as the bridegroom. In other places he may say … "The centre of the soul is God."'[9] Bernard of Clairvaux (twelfth-century), who managed to turn the Song of Solomon into an erotic love story between God and man, described this moment of union as the time when the believer is 'kissed with the kisses of His mouth'.[10] Similar depictions are common in mystical literature.

Pseudo-Dionysius (so called because we don't know his real name but he used Dionysius borrowed from a convert of Paul in Acts 17:34) set the table for the need for this type of mysticism with his belief that God can never be truly known through the intellect. Harkness describes it well,

> The author's position is that God is completely transcendent, beyond all human thought, reason, intellect, or any approaches of the mind. A term, which occurs repeatedly in this writing (*Mystical Theology*), is 'the Divine Dark'. The human mind can only say what God is not, never what God is. There is nothing within the human self to give us a clue. But is there no way to penetrate this divine darkness? Yes, there is one. This is the *via negativa* by which the soul strips off its selfhood and, in ecstatic union with transcendent deity, both feels and knows its oneness with the Infinite. This has become the classic pattern of Christian mysticism. … To this there is often linked a disparagement of the human capacity to know God save by the mystical vision, and to

this end the need of rigorous disciplines of prayer, fasting, prolonged meditation, and ascetic living.[11]

In other words, the mystic has no confidence in human knowledge accessible through normal means such as the propositional revelation of God (Scripture). If we are to know God, it must come from a mystical union with Him that transcends the rational thought process or even normal sensory experience. This takes place through following the three stages of purgation, illumination and union; implementing the spiritual disciplines and most importantly, practicing contemplative prayer. Roman Catholic monk, William Johnston, describes the mystical process this way, 'In this mystical life one passes from one layer to the next in an inner or downward journey to the core of the personality where dwells the great mystery called God.'[12]

Other well-known mystics, holding to these or similar views, throughout church history include: Meister Eckhart, Juliana of Norwich, Thomas à Kempis, Teresa of Ávila, Evelyn Underhill, St. Francis of Assisi, Madam Guyon, George Fox, Thomas Merton and Agnes Sanford. Modern mystics of import include Dallas Willard, Brennan Manning and most importantly, Richard Foster. Of Foster, Eugene Peterson enthusiastically writes on the cover of the 25th anniversary edition of *Celebration of Discipline,* 'Richard Foster has "found" the spiritual disciplines that the modern world stored away and forgot, and has excitedly called us to celebrate them. For they are, as he shows us, the instruments of joy, the way into mature Christian spirituality and abundant life.'

What Foster 'found' many others are discovering as well. As a result classical, medieval Roman Catholic mysticism has been dusted off and offered as the newest and best thing in spirituality. But there is one little problem. If this is how God wanted his followers to connect with him why didn't he bother to say so in his Word? If contemplative prayer (which will be detailed below) is the key that will unlock this greater dimension of spirituality, as we will see is being claimed, why did God not give us instructions on how to pray in this manner? Why did he leave it up to monks and nuns hundreds of years later to unveil this key to true godliness? Of course, the answer is that he did not. God's Word is sufficient;

all that we need for life and godliness is found there (1 Peter 1:4; 2 Tim. 3:16, 17). That brings us to a number of questions: What does the face of modern mysticism look like, where is it leading us and why is it so popular?

The modern face of mysticism

Medieval mysticism has managed to survive within small pockets of Roman Catholicism for centuries but has gone largely unnoticed by evangelicals. It is true that a few groups, such as the Quakers, have always kept some aspect of mysticism within range of evangelical awareness, and elements of mystical practices have actually thrived in charismatic circles right down to the ranks of Fundamentalism. But classical mysticism was virtually unknown in evangelical circles until 1978 when Quaker minister Richard J. Foster published *Celebration of Discipline, the Path to Spiritual Growth*. Hailed by *Christianity Today* as one of the ten best books of the twentieth century and voted by the readers of that magazine as the third most influential book after the Bible, *Celebration of Discipline* has blown the doors off evangelicals' understanding of spirituality. What Foster has done, in essence, is reintroduce to the church the so-called 'masters' of the interior life' as he likes to call the medieval mystics. He declares that they alone have discovered the key to true spiritual life and slowly, over the last few years, convinced multitudes that he is right.

It seems to me that Foster's recipe for Christian living has been simmering in the pot for over two decades but as of late has caught fire. New forces and new players have popularized Foster's ideas to a new set of Christians and it seems to be rapidly taking hold. This is due to the efforts of organizations such as Youth Specialties, numerous Bible colleges, and a rash of books and speakers, all introducing mystical practices and theology to our young people and our young ministers. Many of these, having grown up in churches that no longer major on the teaching of Scripture and are thus lacking biblical discernment, are easy prey for spiritual sounding techniques, especially those that promise such personal and life changing encounters with God. Before we look into the disciples of Foster, we should first get a good overview into Foster's key teachings.

In general

Celebration of Discipline alone, not even referencing Foster's other writings and teachings and ministries, is a virtual encyclopaedia of theological error. We would be hard pressed to find in one so-called evangelical volume such a composite of false teaching. These include faulty views on the subjective leading of God (pp.10, 16-17, 18, 50, 95, 98, 108-109, 128, 139-140, 149-150, 162, 167, 182); approval of new age teachers (see Thomas Merton below); occultic use of imagination (pp.25-26, 40-43, 163, 198); open theism (p.35); misunderstanding of the will of God in prayer (p.37); promotion of visions, revelations and charismatic gifts (pp.108, 165, 168-169, 171, 193); endorsement of rosary and prayer wheel use (p.64); misunderstanding of the Old Testament Law for today (pp.82, 87); mystical journaling (p.108); embracing pop-psychology (pp.113-120); promoting Roman Catholic practices such as use of 'spiritual directors', confession and penance (pp.146-150, 156, 185); and affirming of aberrant charismatic practices (pp.158-174, 198).

However, all of these are minor in comparison to the two main thrusts of Foster's book and ministry that we will get to in a moment, but first who are a few of Foster's mystical champions?

A few mystic heroes

Foster introduces to the unsuspecting reader literally dozens of mystics, some from the Christian tradition, some not. Many of these, he assures us, have travelled to depths of spiritual experience that we moderns cannot even imagine. Foster wants us to know that these individuals knew the secrets to an encounter with God. If only we would follow their pattern we too could enjoy what they enjoyed. Just who are these mystics? Let me give you a thumbnail sketch of three of Foster's favourites.

Meister Eckhart

Eckhart, a Dominican monk who lived in the thirteenth and four-teenth centuries, ranks among the great Roman Catholic mystics such as Teresa of Ávila, John of the Cross, and Julian of Norwich. Toward the end of his life Eckhart was charged (and found guilty after his death in 1327), with heresy for his mystical assertions which the Catholic Church determined had bled over into panthe-ism. Eckhart 'believed that in every human soul there is something of the very nature of God. Here it is that the human soul meets God… [His] doctrine of the human soul has lasted to the present, and is reaffirmed whenever one speaks of a Divine Spark within each of us.'[13] Eckhart made statements such as these, 'Henceforth I shall not speak about the soul, for she has lost her name yonder in the oneness of divine essence. There she is no more called soul: she is called infinite being.' And, 'She plunges into the bottom-less well of the divine nature and becomes one with God that she herself would say that she is God.' Such statements not only both-ered the medieval church but some more modern researchers have found agreements in Eckhart's philosophy with all the major points of Hindu mystics.[14] Other scholars are not so certain about Eck-hart's pantheism but his statements certainly leave the door open for such interpretations. Yet Eckhart is considered to be one of the most important Christian mystics of the middle ages and both ancient and modern mysticism reflect his views. Eckhart's 'Divine Spark' corresponds almost directly with the teachings of Eastern mysticism, with the difference that the Divine Spark in Christian mysticism is defined as God who resides in every human being.

Thomas Merton

Foster cites and/or quotes Merton on at least nine separate occa-sions in *Celebration of Discipline*, yet Merton was not a Christian as far as we can tell. He was a twentieth-century Roman Catholic who had so immersed himself in Buddhism that he claimed he saw no contradiction between Buddhism and Christianity and intend-ed to become as good a Buddhist as he could.[15] But despite his doctrinal views and New Age leanings Foster considers Merton's

Contemplative Prayer, 'A must book',[16] and says of Merton, '[He] has perhaps done more than any other twentieth-century figure to make the life of prayer widely known and understood.'[17] Merton wrote, 'If only [people] could see themselves as they really are. If only we could see each other that way all the time. There would be no more war, no more hatred, no more cruelty, no more greed… I suppose the big problem would be that we would fall down and worship each other.'[18]

Ignatius Loyola

We know Loyola today mainly due to his founding of the Society of Jesus, or the order of the Jesuits in 1534. One of the missions of the Jesuits was to fight the battles of the church against infidels and heretics, in what is now termed the 'Counter-Reformation'. For our purposes, Ignatius' contribution lies in the creation of his *Spiritual Exercises* which provided specifications for spiritual self-examination and the mental and spiritual conditioning of the Jesuits. Foster's disciplines seem to draw heavily upon Ignatius.

St. John of the Cross and Teresa of Ávila are also mystics of note, involved in the sixteenth-century Counter-Reformation seeking to overturn the Reformation. These mystics believed that through contemplation a union with God could be obtained which would eradicate sinful actions and tendencies.

Main teachings

As concerning as many of Richard Foster's teachings and mentors are, far more disturbing are the two main thrusts of his spiritual formation system. The first is his use of what he calls the 'Spiritual Disciplines'. The second is closely related, but deserves its own chapter. I speak of what is called contemplative prayer, which is rapidly becoming the rage throughout much of evangelicalism, especially among the youth.

Spiritual disciplines as a means of grace

It might be best to begin this section by relaying an experience that Foster shares in *Celebration of Discipline*. Having come to the conclusion that there must be 'more spiritual resources than I was experiencing', he prayed,

> Lord, is there more you want to bring into my life? I want to be conquered and ruled by you. If there is anything blocking the flow of your power, reveal it to me.[19]

God seemed to answer this prayer through a growing impression that something in his past was impeding the flow of life so he set aside blocks of time on three consecutive days to listen to God in absolute silence, through the use of journaling, a process whereby God is supposed to reveal his mind to the silent participant. After the third day Foster took his lists to a friend, who volunteered to serve as his confessor, who prayed for healing for all the sorrows and hurts of Foster's past as presumably revealed by God. It was following this experience of journaling, an experience not taught in the Bible but common in the occultic world, that it seemed to him that he 'was released to explore what were for me new and uncharted regions of the Spirit. Following that event, I began to move into several of the Disciplines described in this book that I had never experienced before'.[20]

It is most disturbing that Foster's *magnum opus* stems from a questionable divine encounter of a dubious nature. But it is also significant to realize that Foster's system for spiritual formation is not drawn from the Scriptures but from subjective experiences involving unbiblical methodologies and reinforced by Roman Catholic mystical practices. At the very least this should give pause to any seeker of truth. It must not be automatically assumed, as many seem to do, that Foster has rediscovered the missing jewels of spirituality.

Even more to the point, the dust jacket of this edition assures us 'that it is **only by and through these practices** that the true path to spiritual growth can be found' (emphasis mine). If spiritual growth is dependent upon the spiritual disciplines described in Foster's book, should not we have expected to find this truth in the Scriptures? Why did God reveal them, not to the apostles but to apostate Roman Catholic mystics, and then to Richard Foster as he studied the mystics and used occultic techniques of meditation? We need to tread very carefully through this spiritual minefield. If this is in fact one of the ten best books of the twentieth century, I am not too anxious to read the other nine.

The spiritual disciplines

But just what are the Spiritual Disciplines which are absolutely essential to our spiritual development? Foster breaks them into three categories: inward, outward and corporate. The first two inward disciplines both deal with prayer and will be addressed in the next chapter. Fasting is the third and, as might be expected, his instructions on fasting are purely extra-biblical. The purpose behind fasting, the value of it, and the methodology are interesting, but purely subjective and unauthorative.

The final inward discipline is study. The new reader of Foster might expect that he would direct us to the study of Scripture as the primary means of spiritual growth. But Foster has broader ideas. Actually there are two "books" to be studied: verbal and nonverbal. Verbal books include any literature and one of the important means of study is repetition. Here he sees the use of a rosary and/or Hindu type prayer wheel as being effective (p.64). After a number of suggestions on reading books, Foster finally discusses the type of books to read to enhance spiritual growth. At last, we think he will turn to the Word, and he does — for two paragraphs, before rushing off to recommend reading the medieval mystical classics.

The nonverbal book is mainly the 'reading' of nature. Here with St. Francis he encourages 'making friends with the flowers and trees and the little creatures that creep upon the earth' (p.74). We should also be students of people and of ourselves, and while there is undoubted value in this, many have spent a lifetime studying nature, people and themselves and have no clue about God. Repeatedly we find in Foster that he is just not that interested in the study of Scripture except as it serves his purpose for contemplative meditation.

The outward disciplines begin with simplicity, starting with the simple life as modelled by the heretical cult known as the Shakers. Extreme mystic Thomas Kelly tells us that simplicity allows us to live out of 'The Divine Centre' (whatever that is) and existentialist Kierkegaard claimed it led to holiness. In attempting to find a biblical base for his view, Foster makes the Old Testament civil laws a pattern for New Testament Christianity, and manages to misinterpret virtually every scriptural passage he uses, although he scores points on seeking the kingdom of God first.

Next up is solitude. What follows is not a nice chapter on the importance of breaking free from the noise and distractions of our world and focusing on God and his Word. Instead we enter into the mystical world of Medieval Catholicism, Quakerism and Eastern mystics. Quotes flow from Merton, Teresa of Ávila, John Woolman, George Fox, and St. John of the Cross. Terms like 'The Divine Centre', 'The Divine Opening' and 'the dark night of the soul' dominate. It is here that we are taught to keep a journal as we 'listen to the thunder of God's silence' (p.108).

The next discipline is 'submission' and it is in this chapter that we receive our heaviest dose of psychobabble including: 'self-fulfilment', 'self-actualization', 'loving ourselves', and mutual submission within marriage. To be fair he also explores accurately some of what the Bible teaches on greatness and submission. The final discipline is service, and as with the others this one too is based more on writings of the mystics than on the Scriptures. This is only expected from Foster because he places far more importance on mystical experiences than he does on the Word. For example he writes, 'True service comes from a relationship with the divine Other deep inside. We serve out of whispered promptings, divine urgings' (p.128). But he does warn, 'The *fact* that God speaks to us does not guarantee that we rightly understand the message. We often mix our word with God's word' (emphasis his) (p.140).

Not only does Foster consistently elevate these subjective experiences over the Scriptures, but in this chapter on service Foster recommends self-abasement: 'The strictest daily discipline is necessary to hold these passions in check. The flesh must learn the painful lesson that it has no rights of its own. It is the work of hidden service that will accomplish this self-abasement' (p.131, cf. p.133). This is in direct contradiction to Paul's teaching in Colossians 2:20-23, which tells us that self-abasement has no affect on the passions of the flesh.

The final category of disciplines is the corporate — and here Foster does no better. The first corporate discipline is that of confession; and we are not surprised to discover that Foster supports the position of the Roman Catholic Church, complete with penance and absolution (pp.146-149). And why not? for Dietrich Bonhoeffer assures us that 'when I go to my brother to confess, I am going to God' (p.146), and Foster wants us to know, 'The assurance of forgiveness is sealed in the Spirit when it is spoken by our brother or sister in the name of Christ' (p.148). Since none of this is drawn from Scripture, how can Foster be so sure? Well, not only do his favourite mystics back his view, but so does personal experience. Once when receiving the confession of a lady she, 'looked at me and 'saw' superimposed upon my eyes the eyes of Another who conveyed to her a love and acceptance that released her to unburden her heart' (p.155). While nothing in the Bible remotely implies such an experience we are left to assume that the eyes she saw were the eyes of God. I am not so certain.

As for the discipline of worship, we find that worship 'is a breaking into the Shekinah of God, or better yet, being invaded by the Shekinah of God… We have not worshiped the Lord until Spirit touches spirit… [And] it all begins as we enter the Shekinah of the heart' (pp.158-162). This convoluted understanding of worship is augmented with a strong charismatic flavour. As a matter of fact 'if Jesus is our Leader, miracles should be expected to occur in worship. Healing, both inward and outward, will be the rule, not the exception' (p.165). Such services will have prophecies and words of knowledge (p.165) and that is because, 'The mightiest stirring of praise in the twentieth century has been the charismatic movement. Through it God has breathed new life and vitality into millions' (p.168). But even more disturbing is the idea that in the worship of God, 'Our rational faculties alone are inadequate… That is one reason for the spiritual gift of tongues. It helps us to move beyond mere rational worship into a more inward communion with the Father. Our outward mind may not know what is being said, but our inward spirit understands. Spirit touches spirit' (p.169). Remember above how we have not worshiped until Spirit touches spirit — now we see the process. It is as we move beyond the mind and into mystical, subjective experiences, that true worship takes place.

With all that Foster has already communicated, the discipline of guidance is predictable. 'Many', he tells us, 'Are having a deep and profound experience of an Emmanuel of the Spirit — God with us; a knowledge that in the power of the Spirit Jesus has come to guide his people himself; an experience of his leading that is as definite and as immediate as the cloud by day and the pillar by night' (p.175). The model, of course, of this kind of guidance is the mystic. We are also introduced at this point to the Catholic concept of Spiritual Directors (pp.185-187), something that Foster believes only Roman Catholic monastics know much about today.

Foster brings everything together with his last discipline, that of celebration. Here we are to express joy in all that we have learned thus far in the book, even participation in 'holy laughter' on occasion (p.198).

Robert Webber, professor of theology at Wheaton College illustrates Foster's impact well, 'Over the past two decades my own personal spiritual pilgrimage has taken me away from the propositional and rationalistic mind-set that proclaims an intellectualized proof-oriented faith toward a Christianity of practice and experience' (p.208). Webber is of course erecting a straw man. No one is calling for a purely intellectualized faith devoid of practice and experience. What those who draw their cue from Scripture and not mystics are calling for is a Christian faith, experience and practice that is rational, intellectual, makes sense, and most importantly is solidly grounded on the Word of God. Foster and company have taken many far into the pursuit of mystical experiences that lead to a pseudo-Christianity that has the appearance of spirituality but not the substance.

13

The Challenge of Mysticism: Part II

The heart and soul of mysticism, any type of mysticism, Christian or otherwise, is the art of meditation or contemplation. Georgia Harkness informs us that 'among the church fathers, "contemplation" was the usual term to designate what was later to be called mystical experience'.[1] Contemplative prayer, also known as centring prayer and breath prayer, is rapidly gaining popularity and acceptance in evangelical circles, so it is vital that we understand exactly what is being promoted and why we should be concerned.

What is contemplative prayer?

First we must distinguish between normal prayer and meditation, which is found, recommended, and demanded throughout Scripture and contemplative prayer, which is not. Prayer is our communication with God. The Lord speaks to us through his Word, and we are to carefully meditate on the message given there (Ps. 4:4; 119:15, etc). We speak to him in prayer. Such prayers are rational, intelligent and flow from our minds. Paul said that he would pray with his spirit **and** he would pray with his mind also (1 Cor. 14:15), not either/or. We are to pray without ceasing (1 Thess. 5:17) and in those prayers we are to make our requests known (Phil. 4:6). In prayer we praise God for his known attributes. In prayer we confess specific sins (1 John 1:9). Gibberish, mindless or wordless prayers are not found in the Word, contrary to the charismatics' assertion to the contrary. Similarly contemplative prayer is not of the Scriptural variety; its origin is not the Bible but Eastern and Christian mystics. It should be mentioned that contemplative prayer (often simply called meditation) is the essence of Hinduism and Buddhism and is practiced virtually identically to the Christianized form.

So exactly what is it? It begins with detachment. Richard Foster, in his original 1978 edition of *Celebration of Discipline* wrote, 'Christian meditation is an attempt to empty the mind in order to fill it' (p. 15). Fill it with what? In Eastern religions a person empties his mind in order to become one with the universe (or the Cosmic Mind). In Christian mysticism one empties the mind in order to become one with God, who is found by the way, in ourselves (it is important to keep in mind Meister Eckhart's divine spark found within the soul of each human being). Foster quotes a number of mystics to describe this experience. For example there is Russian mystic Theophan the Recluse who said, "To pray is to descend with the mind into the heart, and there to stand before the face of the Lord, ever-present, all seeing, within you.'[2]

The constant theme of the mystic is that union with God is possible through contemplative prayer, and that union with God is found within us. St. Teresa of Ávila states, 'As I could not make reflection with my understanding I contrived to picture Christ within me.'[3] She is quoted as also saying, "Settle yourself in solitude and you will come upon Him in yourself.'[4] Such statements show why the mystics were accused of pantheism. Silence is a noted feature of contemplation. Catherine de Haeck Doherty writes, "All in me is silent and... I am immersed in the silence of God.'[5] Francis de Dales notes, 'by means of imagination we confine our mind within the mystery on which we meditate'.[6] Imagination is highly important to the mystics.

As Teresa informs us, this is not an endeavour that comes from their understanding. Mystics are hung out in thin air, so to speak, and must make contact with God through imagination rather than through the rational use of their minds. The power of such experience becomes evident as Foster tells us, 'We are to live in a perpetual, inward, listening silence so that God is the source of our words and actions.'[7]

So, through contemplative prayer the person is to empty his mind (detach), then fill it with imaginative experiences with Christ (attach), who we will find in the silence of our souls, resulting in God becoming the source of our words and actions. Sounds attractive to many, even if no such teaching is found in Scripture. But how is it actually practiced?

The techniques

Just how does one go about practicing contemplative prayer? The techniques are identical to those of Eastern religions and so are familiar to most of us through media presentations of TM and yoga. Gary Thomas gives these typical instructions: 'Choose a word (Jesus or Father, for example) as a focus for contemplative prayer. Repeat the word silently in your mind for a set amount of time (say, twenty minutes) until your heart seems to be repeating the word by itself, just as naturally and involuntarily as breathing. But centering prayer is a contemplative act in which you don't do anything; you're simply resting in the presence of God.'[8]

So, the repetition of words or short phrases, a mantra, is key to this experience. What else? While Richard Foster suggests a number of methodologies he says, 'I find it best to sit in a straight chair, with my back correctly positioned in the chair and both feet flat on the floor... Place the hands on the knees, palms up in a gesture of receptivity. Sometimes it is good to close the eyes to remove distractions and center the attention on Christ. At other times it is helpful to ponder a picture of the Lord or to look out at some lovely trees and plants for the same purpose.'[9]

Brennan Manning gives these instructions in his book, *The Signature of Jesus*:

> The first step in faith is to stop thinking about God in prayer...
> Contemplative spirituality tends to emphasize the need for
> a change in consciousness... we must come to see reality differently... Choose a single, sacred word... repeat
> the sacred word inwardly, slowly and often... Enter into the
> great silence of God. Alone in that silence, the noise within
> will subside and the Voice of Love will be heard.[10]

It is apparently the repetition of the mantra that triggers the blank mind. With the mind blank and the heart open to whatever voices or visions that it encounters, accompanied with a vivid imagination, the individual enters into the mystical state. This is the state so prized in mysticism and it is made possible through contemplative prayer. Concerning all of this Foster encourages, 'Though it may sound strange to modern ears, we should without shame enroll as apprentices in the school of contemplative prayer.'[11] By contrast, we search in vain to find any such encouragement or instruction in the Scriptures. We do however find this type of contemplation at the heart of Eastern religions. That is why I find it both bold and revealing that Foster, in his recommendation of Catherine de Haeck Doherty's ministry, actually admit that the title of her book is, *Poustinia: Christian Spirituality of the East for Western Man.*[12]

But is it biblical?

No experience or methodology promoting spirituality can be dismissed or accepted out of hand. Scripture is the final arbitrator and as we have seen Scripture in no way promotes the mysticism that we have been examining. I found the following admission in Winfried Corduan's book, *Mysticism, an Evangelical Option?* to be most interesting. Corduan would not take as strong a stand on the Scriptures as I would and would even see a mild form of mysticism valid for the Christian. But toward the end of his book he raises some important questions and points.

> Set into the context of the New Testament, this aspect of the mystical experience becomes problematic. For it would entail that mystical experience becomes a source of revelation, a private avenue of insight into God and his workings. If so, as Arthur L. Johnson points out, the evangelical commitment to Scripture as the sole source of revelation becomes undermined. "The Scriptures nowhere teach that God gives us any knowledge through 'spiritual experience.' Knowledge of spiritual matters is always linked to God's propositional revelation, the written Word."[13]

Corduan sounds an important alarm. Mysticism, both ancient and modern is chocked full of supposed revelations from God. As a matter of fact, this is the draw — God will personally meet you in the centre of your soul and communicate to you matters far beyond anything found in Scripture. 'Christian meditation, very simply is the ability to hear God's voice and obey his word', Foster tells us.[14] This is no slip of the pen. Foster is not advocating listening to the voice of God in the written revelation of God. He is not even equating 'his word' with the Bible. He is speaking of hearing God's voice outside of the Scriptures, and obeying that revelation. This is one of the greatest dangers of mysticism. Corduan continues.

> We have claimed that mysticism is a very important aspect of New Testament theology [he defines mysticism somewhat differently than in this book]. And yet there is no mystical experience to be sought. There is no truth to be learned through New Testament mysticism. There is no plan of asceticism or meditation to actualize this mystical reality. Rather, there are two important imperatives. The first is, "Believe on the Lord Jesus!" (Acts 16:31). Immediately the realities discussed above are actualized. The second is, "Live... according to the Spirit!" (Rom. 8:5). The point now is to live a life in the light of the fact that those realities are given by God's grace. Christians do not need to seek present realities, but to enjoy them. As they yield to the work of God, the Holy Spirit produces a new supernatural life in them.[15]

This is New Testament spirituality: regeneration and the indwelling, enabling power of the Holy Spirit, all based on the propositional revelation of Scripture. If God had wanted us to encounter Him through mystical practices such as contemplative prayer, why did He not say so? Why did He not give examples and instructions? How could the Holy Spirit inspire the writing of the Scriptures yet forget to include a chapter or two on mysticism, spiritual exercises and mediation of the Eastern variety? Are we to believe that all of this is a great oversight, a huge 'oops' on God's part to have left out such vital instructions on an indispensable experience that is absolutely essential to Christian spirituality? Then, having realized what He had done, are we to believe God, centuries later, revealed this missing ingredient of Christian living to Roman Catholic monks, where it was rejected by the Reformers, only to have Richard Foster reintroduce it all to the twentieth century. This is a bit hard to swallow, but apparently is being accepted by many today.

Modern promoters of mysticism

If the mystical practices that we have been describing were contained in some little corner of the Christian subculture, we have spent far too much time addressing them. But, unfortunately, what was once in a corner has moved mainstream. More and more organizations, colleges, seminaries and authors are proclaiming the superiority of mystical Christianity. And the focus of all this attention seems to be directed toward the young.

For example, in the late 1990s Youth Specialties, the highly influential youth ministry organization, and the San Francisco Theological Seminary teamed up to do a three-year test project to develop an approach to youth ministry, which incorporates contemplative practices. The project was funded by the Lilly Endowment Fund. Mike Yaconelli, co-founder of Youth Specialties, grew interested in contemplative prayer during a spiritually dry time of his life and after reading a book by Henri Nouwen on the subject. Yaconelli and Youth Specialties have now incorporated contemplative prayer and mysticism in their annual pastor's conferences and national youth conventions that reach over 100,000 youth workers each year.[16] Each conference now offers courses on how to develop a contemplative youth ministry, pray the Lectio Divina (an ancient four-step form of contemplative prayer) and walk the prayer labyrinths. Christianity Today's sister publication, Christian Parenting, recently published an article (Fall 2004) promoting the Lectio Divina for young people. 'Christian' singers such as John Michael Talbot boldly endorse contemplative prayer as well as Eastern practices such as Tai Chi and yoga. Without question, former Catholic priest Brennan Manning is steeped in mysticism; yet, Michael W. Smith gives away his books, Michael Card turns to him for advice and named his son after him, Larry Crabb seeks his counsel, Eugene Peterson loves his work, Max Lucado endorses his books, Philip Yancey considers him a good friend,[17] and Mult-nomah and NavPress, evangelical publishers, publish his books. Mysticism and contemplative prayer is seeping into evangelicalism from many sources, and a deluge could very well be in the offing. We need to be prepared to defend the faith against this highly dangerous perversion of biblical Christianity.

Labyrinths

Most evangelical Christians probably would not recognize themselves in the previous discussion of mysticism, but there are subtle influences at work drawing believers in this direction even without their knowledge. While firmly denying any part in classical mysticism, many are actually participating in time-honoured mystical practices. It must be recognized that most are doing this unintentionally, for new opportunities are turning up that seem to defy recognized categories. Some are innocently adopting ancient mystical practices because they are being endorsed by trusted Christian leaders, or even the medical community. The danger is that involvement in some of these things; no matter how pure the motive, may easily lead the participant away from a biblical faith and into the quagmire of subjectivism and mysticism, or at times even into the occult. I will only take time to identify and explain two experiences which are paving the way to mysticism.

I will deal most extensively with labyrinths because they have had a recent resurgence into evangelical circles without sounding many alarms. The Labyrinth Society is only seven years old but boasts 800 members and wide ranging influence. A labyrinth is sort of a maze, some developed with bushes or other vegetation; others created with stones, tiles, wool or even canvas. Labyrinth lovers recoil from the word maze, however, pointing out that 'Labyrinths are not mazes, although in the English language the words labyrinth and maze are frequently confused. Mazes contain cul-de-sacs and dead ends. They have more than one entrance and more than one exit and are designed to make us lose our way; they're a game. Labyrinths have the exact opposite purpose:

they are designed to help us find our way. They have only one path--from the outer edge into the center and back out again.'[18] Labyrinth's sometimes go by handles such as 'Pneuma Labyrinths' or simply 'prayer walks'.

Labyrinths are by no means distinctively Christian. As a matter of fact according to The Rev. Dr. Lauren Artress, President and Founder of Veriditas™, The Voice of the Labyrinth Movement, 'Labyrinth is an ancient pattern found in many cultures around the world. Labyrinth designs were found on pottery, tablets and tiles that date as far back as 4000 years. Many patterns are based on spirals from nature. In Native American culture it is called the Medicine Wheel and Man in the Maze. The Celts described it as the Never Ending Circle. It is also called the Kabala in mystical Judaism. One feature they all share is that they have one path which winds in a circuitous way to the center.'[19]

While the history of labyrinths is sketchy, their entry point into Christianity appears to be during the Middle Ages. Many Christians during that time attempted to make pilgrimage to the Holy City of Jerusalem at some point in their lives but the Crusades made the visits increasingly difficult, if not impossible. Labyrinths were constructed in and around many Catholic cathedrals as a substitute, allowing Christians to fulfil their obligations (some seemed to believe these pilgrimages were necessary for salvation) symbolically.

One of the best known labyrinths was constructed in the early 13th century of tile and inlaid in the floor of the Cartres Cathedral in France. But walking the labyrinth fell out of favour during the 16th and 17th century as the Catholic Church moved away from mysticism and more into rationalism. Until very recently the labyrinth at Cartres was covered with chairs, having not been used for its original purpose for centuries. Rev. Lauren Artress, after a visit to Cartres, brought a replica of the 11-circuit labyrinth back to Grace Cathedral, an Episcopal church in San Francisco in 1992. Since then over a million people are reported to have walked that labyrinth alone, and the labyrinth movement has been given new life. As some walk a labyrinth they claim a feeling of coming home. Others say they recall 'ancient memories', tapping into a level of consciousness not experienced before.

The purpose of labyrinths

All are in agreement that labyrinths are archetypes of the divine which are found in all religious traditions throughout the world. To the leaders of the movement they have rediscovered a long-forgotten mystical tradition. Dr. Artress says that, 'The labyrinth has only one path so there are no tricks to it and no dead ends. The path winds throughout and becomes a mirror for where we are in our lives. It touches our sorrows and releases our joys. Walk it with an open mind and an open heart.'[20] Artress then describes the stages of the walk and the best method for experiencing it.

Three stages of the walk

- Purgation (Releasing) ~ A releasing, a letting go of the details of your life. This is the act of shedding thoughts and distractions. A time to open the heart and quiet the mind.
- Illumination (Receiving) ~ When you reach the centre, stay there as long as you like. It is a place of meditation and prayer. Receive what is there for you to receive.
- Union (Returning) ~ As you leave, following the same path out of the centre as you came in, you enter the third stage,

which is joining God, your Higher Power, or the healing forces at work in the world. Each time you walk the labyrinth you become more empowered to find and do the work you feel your soul reaching for.

Guidelines for the walk

Dr. Artress recommends that the walker, 'quiet your mind and become aware of your breath. Allow yourself to find the pace your body wants to go. The path is two ways. Those going in will meet those coming out. You may "pass" people or let others step around you. Do what feels natural'.[21]

For those who are familiar with classical mysticism of any stripe, you will immediately recognize that labyrinths are merely a tool to move the worshipper into a mystical union with God (as you understand him). And 'as a device, the labyrinth has been compared to, in terms of function, rosaries, Stations of the Cross, and the tao-te-ching, or the Chinese Book of the Way'.[22] Yet, even with all of its obvious connections with various world religions and Medieval Roman Catholicism, some have tried to conjure up biblical support from Jeremiah 6:16, 'Stand at the crossroads, and look, and ask for the ancient paths, where the good way lies; and walk in it, and find rest for your souls.'[23]

All of this would be of little consequence if the labyrinth revival were confined to a few European cathedrals, and a liberal church in San Francisco. The fact is interest in labyrinths have caught fire both inside and out of the evangelical community. The Lighthouse Trails, one Christian watchdog organization which does research on such subjects, reports that a Google search (if you don't know what that is, ask your kids) on labyrinths revealed 116,000 hits in March 2004. But less than a year later a Google search brings up 290,000 hits. More alarming is that labyrinths are rapidly becoming a recognized form of worship in many evangelical organizations and churches. They are being promoted by Youth for Christ, Youth Specialties, Intervarsity Christian Fellowship, The Emergent Church Convention, Navpress, Rick Warren (through his recommendation of Navpress' pro-contemplative magazine, *Discipleship*

Journal and speaking at Youth Specialties conferences), Zondervan Publishing, National Pastors Convention, Leadership Magazine, Group Publishing and a host of others. At the 2004 National Pastors Convention, held in San Diego, the daily morning schedule included: opportunities to walk the labyrinth (from 7 a.m. - 10:30 p.m.); 'Contemplative Morning Prayer Exercise' (8:30 a.m. – 9:15 a.m.); and 'Sustainable Life Forum: Stretching and Yoga' (8:30 a.m. – 9:15 a.m.). Speakers at this convention included Rick Warren, Howard Hendricks, Dan Kimball and Brian McLaren (the latter two are emergent church leaders). Sadly, I have heard of very conservative Bible Colleges offering labyrinth walks to their students, and can only hope that their leadership is ignorant of the true purpose behind the labyrinth.

Visualization

A number of years ago Karen Mains pretty much torpedoed the ministry of Chapel of the Air, her own ministry, and that of David, her husband, when she wrote *Lonely No More*. In that book she chronicled her journey into Jungian psychology, visualization and the occult. She of course denied any involvement with the occult, but judge for yourself.

Mains describes dreams about her 'male-self', a man she called Eddie Bishop. 'He was tall ... well formed and trim, somewhere in his early thirties ... His fine, dark hair fell in a thick lock across his forehead ... his blue-gray eyes looking earnestly into mine.' The details of his communication are specific: '"You are everything I have *ever* wanted spiritually," he said before I [in the dream] started to drive away.' Mains claims that this experience has taken place 'six or eight times a year for the last four or five years'.[24] and has had a 'positively profound effect' on her, compelling her to seek psychospiritual counsel. A later session with her "spiritual director" at Cenacle, a Catholic contemplative retreat centre, Mains tells of a drastic change in the entity which has been appearing in her mind. She describes an "idiot-child sitting at a table with other people. Its head totally bald and lolled to one side. It was drooling and seemed to be six, seven or eight years of age... It was so emaciated and malnourished... He turned his sad, huge *eyes* on me and smiled sweetly... This is my idiot-child, the idiot-self of my self.'[25]

Her 'spiritual director' has her close her *eyes* and *see* the child again. She does so and begins to communicate with the image, who surprises them both by revealing that it is the 'Christ child'. Mrs. Mains ponders the thought that the young man and the idiot-child are both Jesus Christ who has 'been attempting to woo me because an essential part of my identity in Him has been expelled from my adult development'.[26] We find that this 'Christ child', whom she is instructed to always take with her, is her 'spiritual authority' which she is 'afraid of having' and has 'rejected not only [as] a part of myself, but a part of myself that is Christ'.[27]

While she admits that the psychological concept of the male-within-the-female (and vice versa) was developed by Carl Jung, she has always seen it as scriptural.[28] In her self-analysis of her visualized experiences, Mains writes, 'Through my hardships I discover there's a small part of myself that hasn't grown whole along with the rest of me. It's been maimed by neglect during years of married life. I call it my "idiot-self." I'm discovering that this malnourished orphan needs to be nursed and nurtured. I must find the idiot-self creeping about in the infrastructure of my soul... Self of my self, this abandoned child is very much a part of me... I understand that in some way, I, the intuitive, introverted, feeling-proficient female, have become the substitute for [my husband] David's own female self, his anima, to use the Jungian terminology. He... functions for me as my animus... I have abdicated to my husband my own maleness.'[29]

The spiritual path that Karen Mains describes in *Lonely No More* can easily be found in most occult spiritual transformation books.

An uproar ensued following the publication of *Lonely No More* and it was immediately removed from the bookshelves and taken out of print, but not before irreparable damage was done. The people of God were just not ready for a heavy dose of visualization and occultic practices at the time. Fast forward a dozen years and the spiritual landscape is different today, and apparently more primed for such techniques. David Seamand, a frequent guest on such programs as 'Focus on the Family' has written a number of books advocating 'Christian' visualization including, *Healing for Damaged Emotions* and *Healing of Memories.*

Recently, popular author and theologian Gregory Boyd has written a similar book entitled *Seeing Is Believing. Seeing Is Believing* is a good example of how occultic visualization practices are creeping into evangelicalism. Boyd's thesis is that 'it's not what we believe intellectually that impacts us; it's what we experience as real.'[30] Experience is the key word, used literally hundreds of times in this small volume (57 times in the 8 page introduction alone). How does one go about experiencing Jesus? Using 2 Corinthians 3:17-4:6 as his main text, Boyd tells us that imagination, when guided by the Holy Spirit and submitted to the authority of Scripture, is our main receptor to the spiritual world.[31] The problem is that our Western mindset rejects imagination as make believe (pp. 72, 86, 95, 127-128, 134, 205). So it is necessary to reject this worldview and adopt an Eastern, mystical understanding. When this happens we begin to use our imagination to discover the real Jesus.[32]

The most disturbing part of Boyd's imaginative prayer methodology is that it evolves into New Age visualization. Boyd does not deny this; his caveat is that his program should not be condemned through guilt by association.[33] By visualization what we mean is that at some point in this process the image imagined (the spirit-guide in New Age mysticism) actually comes alive and begins to act independently of the person (such as happened with Karen Mains). At that point, contact has been made with the spirit world in ways clearly condemned by Scripture. For example, Boyd gives numerous examples such as this one, 'Sometimes as I rest with the Lord he will say something unexpected like, "Are you ready for more of my freedom?"' Then Jesus leads him to some memory from his past and reconstructs it. This is not wholesome imagination but the altering of reality and contact with the spirit world (he naively assumes the spirit speaking to him is really Jesus). Boyd maintains that only in this manner can a person grow in his knowledge of Christ and/or have his memories healed.[34]

John Weldon and John Ankerberg tell us, 'Visualization is the use of mental concentration and directed imagery in the attempt to secure particular goals, whether physical, psychological, vocational, educational, or spiritual. Visualization attempts to program the mind to discover inner power and guidance. It is often used as a means to, or in conjunction with, altered states of consciousness (for example, as produced by meditation), and is frequently used to develop psychic abilities or make contact with spirits.'[35]

Visualization is being used today not only in the occult but also in New Age medicine in an attempt to manipulate mystical life energies; education to tap the 'higher self' and its powers; psychotherapy and the church, to bring about inner healing.

Visualization must be distinguished from imagination. Healthy imagination is a good and wonderful gift from God, but visualization is something very different. In visualization a person is attempting to either directly alter reality or make contact with the spirit world. Both of these practices are condemned in Scripture. David Hunt distinguishes visualization proper from the nonoccult use of the imagination. He observes:

> The visualization we are concerned with is an ancient witchcraft technique that has been at the heart of shamanism for thousands of years, yet is gaining increasing acceptance in today's secular world and now more and more within the church. It attempts to use vivid images held in the mind as a means of healing diseases, creating wealth, and otherwise manipulating reality. Strangely enough, a number of Christian leaders teach and practice these same techniques in the name of Christ, without recognizing them for what they are.[36]

A practitioner of visualization describes it in this manner:

> Programmed visualization...is the deliberate use of the power of your own mind to create your own reality... there is nothing too insignificant or too grand for you to visualize. Our lives are limited by what we see as possible... A basic rule of visualization is: you can use visualization to have whatever you want, but YOU MUST REALLY, REALLY WANT WHAT YOU VISUALIZE (emphases in original).[37]

Visualization has gained popularity in the Western culture as Eastern mystical thought has invaded and been increasingly accepted. This is true because visualization fits best with a pantheistic worldview that sees humans as divine and creators of their own reality. Visualization is an important technique that supposedly taps the higher self and initiates contact with the ultimate cosmic reality.

By contrast, the Scriptures do not teach or encourage visualization for the healing of memories, healing of body or soul, or spiritual growth. Rather we are called to be renewed daily by the Holy Spirit, prayer and the Word of God.

14

The Challenge of the Emergent Church: Part I

The emergent church is a rather slippery name for a rather slippery movement. By slippery I mean that the movement is so new (originating in the late 1990s), so fragmented, so varied, that nailing it down is like nailing the proverbial JELL-O to the wall. There are no official leaders[1] or headquarters;[2] some have said that there are thousands of expressions yet only a few churches have sold out to the concept; and even those claiming the name can't agree on what is going on.[3] Brian McLaren, the closest thing to a spokesperson for the movement so far, states, 'Right now Emergent is a conversation, not a movement. We don't have a program. We don't have a model. I think we must begin as a conversation, then grow as a friendship, and see if a movement comes of it.'[4]

Having said this, there is still much common ground that can be identified. The name 'emerging church' speaks of a church which is, guess what, emerging from something. This means, it is coming out of the more traditional understanding of the church and emerging into a postmodern expression of the church. What it will actually become is still a matter of speculation, but its adherents see it as a postmodern church for a postmodern culture. Of course, even this gets tricky because the prefix 'post' has become all too trendy. We hear not only of post-modern, but also of post-Christian, post-Protestant, post-analytical, post-liberal, post-conservative, post-everything. The problem with 'post' is that it describes what you *are not* much better than it describes what you *are not*. If you are no longer modern or Christian or liberal or conservative, what are you?

McLaren believes that defining postmodern is premature[5] — we don't yet know what form it will take, so defining the postmodern church is even more problematic. Emergent church leaders do not all agree on where the church goes from here but they all believe that it must go somewhere, for they believe the modern church cannot connect with the postmodern mind. How this fleshes out will be dealt with later in our study; for now we can say the emergent church is a movement chasing a culture.

Dan Kimball, author of *The Emerging Church*, says this is necessary because 'the basis of learning has shifted from logic and rational, systematic thought to the realm of experience. People increasingly long for the mystical and the spiritual rather than the evidential and facts-based faith of the modern soil'.[6]

Kimball suggests that the seeker-sensitive church, the church that chased the last generation's culture, is already out of date: 'The things that seeker-sensitive churches removed from their churches are the very things [postmodern] nonbelievers want to experience if they attend a worship service.'[7] The postmodern wants to reconnect to the past. They want traditions and religious symbols rather than slick excellence, polished performance and state-of-the art structures found in modernity. That translates into a very different look and feel. For example it is not likely that you will find a sign along the highway pointing to the First Baptist Emergent Church. Names like Baptist and denominational ties are too modernistic. Popular emergent church names are Solomon's Porch, House of Mercy, The Rock, Jacob's Ladder, Circle of Hope, Ikon, Vintage Faith, New Beginnings, Sanctuary, Sanctus and Mosaic. They sponsor websites like vintagefaith.com, emergentvillage.org, and theooze.com. The emerging church appears to be the latest flavor of the day in a church age which allows itself to be defined by its culture rather than by Scripture. D. A. Carson reminds us:

What drove the Reformation was the conviction, among all
its leaders, that the Roman Catholic Church had departed

from Scripture and had introduced theology and practices that were inimical to genuine Christian faith. In other words, they wanted things to change, not because they perceived that new developments had taken place in the culture so that the church was called to adapt its approach to the new cultural profile, but because they perceived that new theology and practices had developed in the church that contravened Scripture, and therefore that things needed to be reformed by the Word of God. By contrast, although the emerging church movement challenges, on biblical grounds, some of the beliefs and practices of evangelicalism, by and large it insists it is preserving traditional confessionalism by changing the emphases because the culture has changed, and so inevitably those who are culturally sensitive see things in a fresh perspective. In other words, at the heart of the emerging reformation lies a perception of a major change in culture.[8]

How does the Christian community go about chasing down the culture? Either through methods or message. The emerging church does both. Beginning with methodology, the leaders of the movement view the under-thirty generations as profoundly spiritual. They are interested in religious experiences and feelings. They want a sense of the supernatural. They are not interested in systematic theology, tightly woven apologetic arguments or logical reasoning. But they are attracted to spiritual mystery. Kimball quotes Garrison Keillor, who makes no claim of being a Christian, as saying, 'If you can't go to church and at least for a moment be given transcendence, if you can't pass briefly from this life into the next, then I can't see why anyone would go. Just a brief moment of transcendence causes you to come out of the church a changed person.'[9]

Despite the fact that Keillor could not be more wrong if we are interested in true biblical transformation, the emergent leaders see this as the gateway to reaching the postmodern generations. The Baby Busters (born between 1965 and 1983) and Mosaics (born between 1984 and 2002) are tired of 'church-lite', consumer spirituality, church buildings that look like warehouses or malls,

CEO pastors, educational programs structured like community colleges and church services that are reminiscent of a Broadway musical. They want the transcendent, as Keillor says.

So the emergent church loads up on such things. There is a return to what Kimball calls the 'vintage church' which combines some excellent things such as singing of hymns, display of the cross and reading of Scripture with (questionable at best) medieval ritual, prayer stations, labyrinths, candles, incense, icons, stained glass, contemplative prayer, mantras, Benedictine chants, and darkness.

Kimball makes the point that postmoderns want to experience God with all five senses — as the vintage church did. It should be pointed out, however, that the vintage church to which Kimball refers is not a return to the New Testament church. The vintage church has been waylaid by medieval Catholicism, which we must remember may have experienced the spiritual through the senses, but nevertheless was an apostate religion. Simply providing an unbeliever with a religious experience, which they might interpret as an encounter with God, may do them more harm than good. But just as the seeker-sensitive church saw felt-needs as the means of linking with unbelievers, so the emerging church sees spiritual experience as that means. The philosophy is basically the same, just the methods have changed.

Emergent leader Leonard Sweet describes the emergent church with the acronym EPIC. 'E' stands for experiential because postmoderns desire more than listening and thinking. They want to enter into worship as an experience of the senses. This is why medieval rituals appeal to them. 'P' speaks of participants as opposed to observers. They want an active faith. Rather than a sermon they might hold a 'conversation'. 'I' relates to image-based. Projected images, artwork, film and video are all attractive to this generation. They are sight-oriented. 'C' means communal. They desire a strong sense of community. They are 'people' persons. Instead of going to church they want to be the church.[10] There are some good things here but there are problems in the details, as we will see.

If this were the end of the story we might even find comfort in what is basically a reaction to the stripped-down model of Christianity that the seeker-sensitive church has given us for the last few decades. But as Rob Bell is quick to inform us, 'This is not just the same old message with new methods. We're rediscovering Christianity as an Eastern religion, as a way of life.'[11] This is something new in the cultural-identifying churches. The seeker-sensitive church loudly proclaimed that they were fine-tuning the methodology but were not tampering with the message of the evangelical church (even though they were). The emergent church is concerned about methods but they are even more concerned about the message. They believe that conservative evangelical Christianity has it all wrong. From the Scriptures to essential doctrines to the gospel itself, the church so far just doesn't get it. And the emergent people include themselves in the same camp. As Brian McLaren states, 'I don't think we've got the gospel right yet. What does it mean to be saved?... None of us have arrived at orthodoxy.'[12]

Emergent Philosophy

Before we jump into the doctrinal distinctive of the emerging church we must first detail the philosophy that undergirds the movement. What we see, read and perceive is filtered, at least to some degree, through our presuppositions and worldview. The worldview of the emerging church is decidedly postmodern. Attempting to combine postmodern philosophy with biblical theology is a tricky business, as one might imagine; we should not be surprised that unanimity in the understanding of this attempted merger will not be found. Nevertheless, some common threads are evident throughout the movement.

Truth Claims

Truth claims are held with suspicion within postmodernism and we find a precarious juggling act in emergent circles as they try to reach a wary culture with the claims of Christ. The emerging church is concerned about presenting genuine Christianity in a way the postmodern culture understands. Since the very heart of postmodernity is rejection of absolute authoritative truth, yet Christianity claims to be the proclamation of absolute authoritative truth, a head-on collision is almost unavoidable. What is to be done? Something has to give and that something seems to be truth. McLaren presents their view:

> Ask me if Christianity (my version of it, yours, the Pope's, whoever's) is orthodox, meaning true, and here's my honest answer: a little, but not yet. Assuming by Christianity you mean the Christians understanding of the world and God, Christian opinions on soul, text, and culture…I'd have to say that we probably have a couple of things right, but a lot of things wrong, and even more spreads before us unseen and unimagined. But at least our eyes are open! To be a Christian in a generously orthodox way is not to claim to have the truth captured, stuffed, and mounted on the wall.[13]

This is almost a complete capitulation to postmodernity's concept of truth. After 2000 years of the study of the completed Canon, we Christians find ourselves in a position of having maybe a 'couple' of things right — and I am sure that those couple of things would be up for grabs. This uncertainty about the truth carries over to the Scriptures themselves, of course. Rob Bell and his wife Kristen, in an interview with *Christianity Today*, reflect this view. They started questioning their assumptions about the Bible itself — 'discovering the Bible as a human product'.[14] 'I grew up thinking that we've figured out the Bible', Kristen says, 'that we knew what it means. Now I have no idea what most of it means, and yet I feel like life is big again — like life used to be black and white, and now it's in color.'[15] To the postmodern mind it is more important to, as Rob Bell says, 'embrace mystery, rather than conquer it'.[16]

But how does a truly postmodern Christian live? How do they know what to believe? How do they deal with the issue of truth? How do they assimilate the realities of life? By creating their own reality. McLaren, if he could have his emergent dream come true, would 'help students construct their own model of reality, their understanding of the universe and story we find ourselves in. And — this is SO important — we'd teach them that their model isn't reality; it's just a model. It must be open to correction, adjustment, improvement, even revolution' (emphasis his).[17] Experience, not Scripture, becomes the basis for truth. 'People today', Leonard Sweet writes, 'are starved not for doctrines but for images and relationships and stories'.[18]

There is no absolute truth or ultimate reality in the emergent agenda. Even Scripture is appreciated for its mystery, not its presentation of truth. Yet one has to wonder what Jude had in mind when he wrote, 'I find it necessary to write to you appealing that you contend earnestly for the faith which was once for all handed down to the saints' (verse 3). The emergent church leaders are asking us to embrace a faith without truth, a Bible which has value due to its mystery, and a reality that is individual, subjective and changeable. This is touted as a new and improved version of Christian living. I fail to see the attraction, not to mention that no such understanding of truth is supportable by the Scriptures.

Deconstruction

The scholar would define deconstruction as Carson does:

> It has to do with a literary approach, that hunts down tensions and inconsistencies in a text (those who deploy deconstruction insist that all texts have them) in order to set them at odds with each other and thus deconstruct the text, to generate new insights that might actually contradict what a text ostensibly says.[19]

At the other end of the spectrum, Humpty Dumpty gave his version, 'When I use a word, it means what I choose it to mean – neither more nor less.'[20] In everyday language deconstruction means that we can never be certain that we have the right interpretation of words. What matters then is not what the author or speaker said, because that doubtfully can be discerned; rather the important thing is what did the reader/listener experience. Deconstruction guts words of their meaning and redefines them according to one's own preference. This is obviously convoluted but it is a central piece in postmodern thought.

How does this work out in the postmodern church? In order to be consistent with absolute truth (or, better, lack of truth) the emergent thinkers must dispose of dogmatic truth claims (i.e. doctrines). They must purge the church of an exclusive gospel,[21] an authoritative Bible and irritating doctrines such as hell.[22] Also on the cutting floor is the doctrine of original sin. McLaren writes,

> The church latched on to that old doctrine of original sin like a dog to a stick, and before you knew it, the whole gospel got twisted around it. Instead of being God's big message of saving love for the whole world, the gospel became a little bit of secret information on how to solve the pesky legal problem of original sin.[23]

Before the emergent church leaders are done all the essential teachings of the Bible have been deconstructed, redefined or dismissed. And what has been put in their place? Oddly, but consistent with postmodern thinking, nothing but mystery and questions. Even McLaren admits, 'What will appear beyond the deconstruction remains to be seen. Perhaps something better will emerge – that is my hope and prayer, but the outcome is by no means certain even now that I have finished writing this book.'[24]

Pluralistic Relativism

If nobody is right then everybody is right. This is the logical conclusion of the postmodern worldview. The emergent church thinkers are reluctantly willing to accept this concept, at least for a time. McLaren states:

> Because I and others, while we aren't 'for' pluralistic relativism, do see it as a kind of needed chemotherapy. We see modernity with its absolutisms and colonialisms and totalitarianisms as a kind of static dream... In Christian theology, this anti-emergent thinking is expressed in systematic theologies that claim ... to have final orthodoxy nailed down... Emergent Christians see pluralistic relativism as a

dangerous treatment for stage 4 absolutist/colonial/totalitarian modernity (to use language from cancer diagnosis), something that saves a life by nearly killing it.[25]

Since truth and Scripture have been deconstructed all that is left is relativism. Until we figure out where to go from here we will have to be content with that. We may or may not arrive at a better place some day, but at least objective truth claims are being eradicated — and that is a good thing. So says the emergent church leaders.

15

The Challenge of the Emergent Church: Part II

Our worldview will determine how we process information and in turn what we believe. In theory, at least, Christians should possess a biblical worldview shaped by the study of Scripture. In actuality, too often our philosophy of living (worldview) is formed by other forces around us including our culture. This is an accusation often cast at the evangelical church by the emerging church leaders. They say that evangelicalism has been shaped by modernity —that what we believe is not drawn so much from Scripture as it is from the Enlightenment. This indictment should not be cast aside too quickly; there is some truth to it. We must ever be careful that we trace our beliefs to Scripture and not take detours constructed by men. But having read the specific allegations coming from the emerging camp, I find that most do not hold water and are thrown out more to put us on the defensive and justify their beliefs than to accurately portray the teachings of the conservative church. When the smoke has cleared we discover that our fundamental doctrines find their basis in Scripture after all. But the same cannot be said for emergent teachings. Their doctrines have been more than tainted; they have been fashioned by postmodernity. Let's take a look through the lens of emergent philosophy at some of the major doctrines.

Emergent Doctrine

In General

Al Mohler, theologian and president of Southern Baptist Seminary in Louisville, Kentucky, provides this scathing comment:

> The worldview of postmodernism — complete with an epistemology that denies the possibility of or need for propositional truth — affords the movement an opportunity to hop, skip and jump throughout the Bible and the history of Christian thought in order to take whatever pieces they want from one theology and attach them, like doctrinal post-it notes, to whatever picture they would want to draw.[1]

Most emergent church leaders claim fidelity to the Scriptures as well as the historic doctrines and even creeds of the church. Sounds good on the surface — but then they force these things through the filter of postmodern deconstruction and what comes out are distorted and unrecognizable understandings of theology. Dan Kimball says that the church must 'deconstruct, reconstruct, and redefine biblical terms'.[2] Brian McLaren would agree, saying that our old theological systems are flawed and something new is needed.

> I meet people along the way who model for me, each in a different way, what a new kind of Christian might look like. They differ in many ways, but they generally agree that the old show is over, the modern jig is up, and it's time for something radically new... Either Christianity itself is flawed, failing, untrue, or our modern, Western, commercialized, industrial strength version is in need of a fresh look, a serious revision.[3]

Rob Bell chips in to make certain we understand that these men are talking about more than methodology, 'By this I do not mean cosmetic, superficial changes like better lights and music, sharper graphics, and new methods with easy-to-follow steps. I mean theology: the beliefs about God, Jesus, the Bible, salvation, the future. We must keep reforming the way the Christian faith is defined, lived and explained.'[4]

How far is Bell willing to take all of this? Which doctrines can be changed, altered or even eliminated before we no longer have the Christian faith? Apparently nothing is off limits. While personally claiming to affirm historic Christian theology, Bell writes that it would not bother him to discover that we have been wrong all along concerning the basic elements of the faith. For example, if it could be proven 'that Jesus had a real, earthly, biological father named Larry... and that the virgin birth was just a bit of mythologizing the Gospel writers threw in... Could you still be a Christian?'[5] Bell doesn't see a problem. As a matter of fact, if our faith depends on such doctrines 'then it wasn't that strong in the first place, was it?'[6]

What doctrines does Bell regard as dispensable? In this brief statement alone he sees as superfluous the virgin birth, the incarnation, the hypostatic union of Christ and the inspiration of Scripture (since the Gospel writers lied about the person of Christ). Of course, like dominos, as these doctrines fall they take others with them, not the least of which would be the substitutionary atonement since a mere man could not die for our sins. In one stroke of the pen Bell has undermined the whole Christian faith, but he sees it as a non-issue. To Bell, and other emergent leaders, Jesus is not the way and the truth, if by that we mean he is the embodiment of truth and the only way to God. No, to these men the 'way of Jesus is the best possible way to live'.[7] We could continue to live the 'Christian life' without the truth of Scripture. We could still love God and be a Christian, because what we believe is not important. The only question is, 'Is the way of Jesus still the best possible way to life?'[8] It is not about what we believe, Bell would insist. 'Perhaps a better question than who's right, is who's living rightly?'[9]

McLaren reinforces this major tenant of emergent 'theology': 'We place less emphasis on whose lineage, rites, doctrines, structures, and terminology are right and more emphasis on whose actions, service, outreach, kindness, and effectiveness are good.'[10] 'A turn from doctrines to practices'[11] is one of the four major legs that the emerging church stands on, according to McLaren. Being, rather than believing, is a major component in the emergent philosophy. The New Testament, on the other hand, does not sacrifice one for the other. We are called in Scripture to live godly lives, but first we must believe (John 1:12; Rom. 10:9-10; Eph. 2:8-9). Christlike living is a fruit of salvation, not the cause. We can 'be' moral and decent people and not be Christians, but we cannot deny or ignore the true historic, biblical person and work of Jesus Christ and be saved. The emergent church has turned this truth on its head. Mark Oestreicher, president of Youth Specialties, makes these comments in *The Emerging Church* which are not only dangerously close to a denial of the gospel itself but actually cross the line:

> Does a little dose of Buddhism thrown into a belief system somehow kill off the Christian part? My Buddhist cousin, except for her unfortunate inability to embrace Jesus, is a better 'Christian' (based on Jesus' descriptions of what a Christian does) than almost every Christian I know. If we are using Matthew 26 (sic.) as a guide, she'd be a sheep; and almost every Christian I know personally would be a goat.[12]

Some emerging churches go even further. Sanctus1, an emerging church in Manchester, England, hosted a 'conversation' called 'blah...manchester' on 11 January 2006. They stated on their blog:

> Churches in the West are increasingly experimenting with more symbolic, reflective spiritualities, drawing from Orthodox and Celtic traditions, and using digital technologies and ambient music. How far can we engage with the Eastern spiritualities of our Sikh, Hindu and Muslim neighbors whilst retaining our Christian integrity? What might an emerging church look like in a multi-faith context?[13]

The key note speaker at this conversation was Pall Singh who leads an organization called Sanctuary which claims to be a, 'faith and grace community gathering for British Asians and others to explore Christ; a safe place where people can experience God's love, acceptance and forgiveness'.[14] At Sanctuary 'We believe that people of all faiths are created in the image of God and are on a spiritual journey of discovery, needing space to experience the grace and truth...'[15]

A Few Specifics

The doctrine of God: Even though Jesus has come to reveal and explain the Father (John 1:14, 18), 'God', McLaren insists, 'can't ever really be an object to be studied.'[16] To emergent leaders theology is not a matter of knowing God but a quest for beauty and truth.

The doctrine of original sin: McLaren writes, 'Many of us have grown uneasy with this understanding of "the fall" (and with it an exaggerated understanding of the doctrine of "original sin"). We are suspicious that it has become a kind of Western Neo-Platonic invasive species that ravages the harmonious balance inherent in the enduring Jewish concepts of creation as God's world.'[17]

The substitutionary atonement: One of the characters in McLaren's book *The Story We Find Ourselves In* goes beyond questioning the purpose and need of Christ's death for us, or even the unfairness of one dying for others. 'That just sounds like one more injustice in the cosmic equation. It sounds like divine child abuse. You know?'[18]

The TULIP: You don't have to be a Calvinist to find McLaren's deconstruction of the famous TULIP ridiculous. The acronym has historically stood for total depravity, unconditional election, limited atonement, irresistible grace, and the perseverance of the saints. McLaren says he too is a Calvinist but he comes up with his own TULIP: Triune love, unselfish election, limitless reconciliation, inspiring grace and passionate, persistent saints.[19]

When deconstructing and reconstructing takes place at this level it is not hard to understand the difficulty involved in communication. As Al Mohler wrote recently on his blog,

> McLaren claims to uphold 'consistently, unequivocally and unapologetically' the historic creeds of the church, specifically the Apostles' and Nicene Creeds. At the same time, however, he denies that truth should be articulated in propositional form, and thus undercuts his own 'unequivocal' affirmation.[20]

The doctrine of hell

So odious is the doctrine of hell to the emergent community that McLaren devoted his latest book, *The Last Word and the Word after That*, to the subject. McLaren introduces his subject with an exaggerated distortion of the evangelical position,

> God loves you and has a wonderful plan for your life, and if you don't love God back and cooperate with God's plans in exactly the prescribed way, God will torture you with unimaginable abuse, forever – that sort of thing. Human parents who "love" their children with these kinds of implied ultimatums tend to produce the most dysfunctional families...[21] (emphasis his).

If the idea of hell is so ridiculous then why did Jesus teach it? McLaren concocts a fanciful view that the Jews during the intertestamental period wove together the mythological views of the Mesopotamian, the Egyptian, the Zoroastrian and Persian religions and created hell. When Jesus came on the scene the Pharisees were using hell as a club to keep the people in line. Through the threat of hell the Pharisees could motivate sinners to stop sinning and then perhaps God would send the Messiah along with His kingdom. Jesus takes the Pharisees' club and turns it on them. Jesus didn't really believe in or endorse hell, as we understand it; he just used it as a 'truth-depicting model'.[22] Jesus used hell 'to threaten those who excluded sinners and other undesirables, showing that God's righteousness was compassionate and merciful, that God's kingdom welcomed the undeserving, that for God there was no out-group'.[23]

This convoluted argumentation leads to there being 'no out-group'. If there is no out-group, does that mean McLaren is a universalist? While he flirts with this possibility stating, 'Universalism is not as bankrupt of biblical support as some suggest',[24] he never firmly lights on it.[25] But without question McLaren does hold to the doctrine of inclusivism which teaches that while salvation has been made possible by Jesus Christ, it is not necessary to know who Jesus is or the precise nature of what he has done.[26] Emergent church leaders follow the reasoning of missionary theologian Lesslie Newbigin's position concerning Christ and salvation which runs along these lines: Exclusive in the sense of affirming the unique truth of the revelation of Jesus Christ, but not in the sense of denying the possibility of salvation to those outside the Christian faith; inclusive in the sense of refusing to limit the saving grace of God to Christian, but not in the sense of viewing other religions as salvific.[27] In other words, salvation is not exclusively found in the gospel, therefore there are saved Hindus, Muslims, Buddhists and so forth. Soon hell becomes a moot issue because no one seems to be going there anyway.

The doctrine of salvation

The doctrine of hell is determined to a large degree by the all-important understanding of the gospel. The emergent leaders see a wide gate opening to eternal life. 'It bothers me to use *exclusive* and *Jesus* in the same sentence. Everything about Jesus' life and message seemed to be about inclusion, not exclusion',[28] writes McLaren (emphasis his). He adds later in his discussion, 'Maybe God's plan is an opt-out plan, not an opt-in one. If you want to stay out of the party, you can. But it's hard for me to imagine somebody being more stubbornly ornery than God is gracious.'[29] The clear implication is that we are all 'in' unless we want 'out'. But the next question is (and this is where it gets tricky) in or out of what? The short answer is 'the kingdom of God'. But the short answer leads to a long explanation that leaves us scratching our heads (which is appropriate since the emergent people prize mystery over clarity).

The gospel, according to the emergent thinkers, is not about individual conversion. It is not about how to get people 'in'. It is about 'how the world will be saved from human sin and all that goes with it...'[30] This sounds close to the mark until we examine more thoroughly what is meant by the terminology. Their concept of 'world' does not simply involve humans who don't believe in Christ. The emergent gospel is not just bringing unbelievers to the Saviour for the forgiveness of sin and the imputation of God's righteousness. There is more, as Rob Bell informs us,

> Salvation is the entire universe being brought back into harmony with its maker. This has huge implications for how people present the message of Jesus. Yes, Jesus can come into our hearts. But we can join a movement that is as wide and as big as the universe itself. Rocks and trees and birds and swamps and ecosystems. God's desire is to restore all of it.[31]

McLaren continues the thought: 'Is getting individual souls into heaven the focal point of the gospel? I'd have to say no, for any number of reasons. Don't you think that God is concerned about saving the whole world?... It is the redemption of the world, the stars, the animals, the planets, the whole show.'[32] You see, 'The church exists for the world – to be God's catalyst so that the world can receive and enter God's kingdom more and more.'[33] When asked to define the gospel, Neo (the main philosophical character in McLaren's novels) replies that it could not be reduced to a little formula, other than 'the Kingdom of God is at hand'.[34] Narrowing this definition is not easy, but McLaren gives some insight when he writes,

> I am a Christian because I believe that, in all these ways, Jesus is saving the world. By the 'world' I mean planet Earth and all life on it, because left to ourselves, un-judged, un-forgiven, and un-taught, we will certainly destroy this planet and its residents.[35]

As we are discovering, the emerging church is very troubled with the planet, with the ecosystems, pollution and the environment; so much so that apparently in some sense Christ died for the physical planet and it is the job of the follower of Christ to help restore and protect this world. He is also concerned with injustice. McLaren asks, 'And could our preoccupation with individual salvation from hell after death distract us from speaking prophetically about injustice in our world today?'[36] Emergent leaders have a deep concern that if we are preoccupied with who is 'in' and who is 'out', who is going to heaven and who is not, we will ignore present physical needs of the planet and social issues like injustice, poverty and AIDS.

McLaren argues, 'When Matthew, Mark, and Luke talk about the Kingdom of God, it's always closely related to social justice… The gospel of the kingdom is about God's will being done on earth for everybody, but we're interested in getting away from earth entirely as individuals, and into heaven instead.'[37] Martin Luther King is given by McLaren as an example of one who had the right gospel emphasis.[38] They fault the evangelical church for being too wrapped up in eternity to care about what is happening right now on planet earth and with being too anxious over who is saved from sin to notice who is suffering from man's inhumanity to man.

It does not seem to be an option to the emergent church that both social injustices and eternal redemption can be and have been attended to by God's people. But, despite opinions to the contrary, the priority of Scripture is on man's relationship to God. It is because men are alienated from God that they mistreat one another. The spiritually redeemed and transformed person should and will care about social sins. But, again, the gospel is about man's alienation from God and what He has done through Christ to reconcile us to himself (Rom. 5:6-11), not about the ozone layer and elimination of poverty. Neither Jesus nor the apostles made these latter things the focus of their ministries; it was the reconciliation of souls to God that was at the heart of their message. Once we begin to draw our gospel from the culture, no matter what culture that might be, we have altered the true gospel. Emergent leaders are not wrong to be concerned about the environment and social injustice; they are wrong to confuse it with the gospel of Jesus Christ.

How those professing to be believers understand the message of the gospel will determine how they view their mission in this life. Since the emergent church sees the gospel not merely as the redemption of lost souls but also as the restoration of the planet and salvation from man's inhumanity to man, they comprehend their task as Christians differently from that of most evangelicals. They call it 'missional'.

Emergent Mission: Missional

Missional is a term that seems to be drawn from the writings of missiologist Lesslie Newbigin who pops up all over emergent literature. It is difficult to pin down a good definition of missional, but it seems to mean that as Christians we exist to serve. We serve by loving and living in such a way that we bless those around us. But more than that, we are to be engaged in changing and even creating culture as we bring the kingdom of God to earth. Rather than calling people out of this world system and into 'the kingdom of His beloved Son' (Col. 1:13), we are to bring the kingdom to them. It would appear that the goal of the missional Christian is to transform the 'domain of darkness' (Col. 1:13) into the kingdom of God. McLaren tells us that his missional calling is summed up in these words, 'Blessed in this life to be a blessing to everyone on earth.'[39] He adds, 'My mission isn't to figure out who is already blessed, or not blessed, or unblessable. My calling is to be blessed so I can bless everyone.'[40] Further,

> From this understanding we place less emphasis on whose lineage, rites, doctrines, structures, and terminology are right and more emphasis on whose actions, service, outreach, kindness, and effectiveness are good... [In order] to help our world get back on the road to being truly and wholly good again, the way God created it to be... We're here on a mission to join God in bringing blessing to our needy world. We hope to bring God's blessing to you, whoever you are and whatever you believe, and if you'd like to join us in this mission and the faith that creates and nourishes it, you're welcome.[41]

We get a better understanding of where McLaren is headed when he writes, 'I hope that both they (people everywhere) and I will become better people, transformed by God's Spirit, more pleasing to God, more of a blessing to the world, so that God's kingdom... comes on earth as in heaven.'[42] And what kind of people will populate this kingdom? Apparently people from all faith and religions.

> Although I don't hope all Buddhists will become (cultural) Christians, I do hope all who feel so called will become Buddhist followers of Jesus; I believe they should be given that opportunity and invitation. I don't hope all Jews or Hindus will become members of the Christian religion. But I do hope all who feel so called will become Jewish or Hindu followers of Jesus.[43]

It doesn't take long to realize that the kingdom of the emergent community is not the kingdom of God, nor the church, as described in Scripture — unless the missional mandate is to fill the kingdom with tares (Matt. 13:24-30, 36-43). But once this unbiblical view of God's kingdom is accepted, what is our mission—that is, how do we live missionally?

Rob Bell writes, 'For Jesus, the question wasn't how do I get into Heaven? but how do I bring heaven here?... The goal isn't escaping this world but making this world the kind of place God can come to. And God is remaking us into the kind of people who can do this kind of work.'[44] Dan Kimball adds, 'Our faith also includes kingdom living, part of which is the responsibility to fight locally and globally for social justice on behalf of the poor and needy. Our example is Jesus, who spent His time among the lepers, the poor and the needy.'[45]

These quotes give good examples of half truths twisted into distorted vision. Did Jesus show compassion and minister to the poor? Certainly, but did Jesus, or the apostles after him, fight for social justice on behalf of the poor and needy? Not at all. While Jesus, through the transformation of lives, began a process that would revolutionize much of the world in regard to injustice, he never made these things a central platform of his ministry nor that of the church. Jesus said virtually nothing about the environment, political tyranny, eradication of poverty and illiteracy, elimination of deadly disease or other social ills. This does not mean that these things are not important, but they are obviously not the heart of His ministry which was to save us from our sins and enable us 'to become the righteousness of God in Christ' (2 Cor. 5:21). Jesus could have started a social revolution without going to the cross, but without the cross we could not be redeemed from sin. Our mission is to call people 'out of darkness into His marvelous light' (1 Peter 2:9).

But the missional agenda is different. Here we are to bless people, for that is why God has chosen us – to be a blessing to others.[46] What does it mean to be a blessing? Apparently it does not mean coming to saving faith in Christ, because Bell tells us that 'God blesses everybody. People who don't believe in God. People who are opposed to God. People who do violent, evil things. God's intention is to bless everybody.'[47] And how does this blessing happen? It happens as the church gives up its efforts to convert people to Christ and simply serves them: 'The most powerful things happen when the church surrenders its desire to convert people and convince them to join. It is when the church gives itself away in radical acts of service and compassion, expecting nothing in return, that the way of Jesus is most vividly put on display.'[48] In this way (Bell tells us) the 'gospel is good news, especially for those who don't believe it… [As a matter of fact] if the gospel isn't good news for everybody, then it isn't good news for anybody.'[49]

But is the gospel good news for everybody? It may very well be a blessing to have Christian people treat you with the love of Christ, but Jesus and the Scriptures could not be more clear that those who do not know Christ are under the wrath of God (Rom. 1:18ff), will perish (2 Thess. 2:9), are eternally doomed (Luke 12:46-48) and will spend eternity in the lake of fire (Rev. 20:11-15) — hardly good news to those who reject him.

Emergent Scripture

Many of the unusual positions held by the emergent leaders stem directly from their theology of the Scriptures as well as their herme-neutical approach. First, insiders of the emerging church 'conver-sation' are fond of expressing their excitement and fidelity to the Word of God, even as they undermine it. McLaren says, 'I want to affirm that my regard for Scripture is higher than ever.'[50] Bell tells us that for over ten years he has oriented his life around studying, reading, and trying to understand the Bible.[51] One would have to wonder why Bell devotes so much time to the understanding of the Bible since he apparently agrees with his wife who stated in a joint interview that she has 'no idea what most of it means. And yet life is big again.'[52]

In order to press home their views, the emergent leaders must perform some interesting gymnastics with the Scriptures. How can someone express high regard for Scripture yet come up with such fanciful interpretations? First, they question inspiration. Wondering out loud about Paul's epistles, Bell writes, 'A man named Paul is writing this, so is it his word or God's Word?'[53] McLaren pulls out the old Jesus versus Paul card, 'We retained Jesus as Savior but promoted the apostle Paul (or someone else) to Lord and Teach-er... And/or decided that Jesus' life and teachings were completely interpreted by Paul.'[54] Bell, in complete ignorance of history and the doctrine of biblical preservation, informs his readers that the canon came about as a result of a vote of the church fathers: 'In re-action to abuses by the church, a group of believers during a time called the Reformation claimed that we only need the authority of the Bible. But the problem is that we got the Bible from the church voting on what the Bible even is.'[55]

Anyone still clinging tenaciously to the Word, after inspiration is denied, will further loosen his grip when he discovers that the Scriptures are not inerrant, infallible nor authoritative. McLaren said these are words related to a philosophical belief system that he used to hold. But he no longer believes the 'Bible is absolutely equivalent to the phrase "the Word of God" as used in the Bible. Although I do find the term inerrancy useful... I would prefer to use the term inherency to describe my view of Scripture.'[56] By the use of inherency he is dusting off the neo-orthodox view of the Scriptures, which taught that the Bible becomes the 'word of God' but is not the completed Word of God, for God's Word can be found in anything he 'inspires'.

If you have any confidence left in Scripture at this point, McLaren and his friends can take care of that by telling you that you have been misreading the Bible all along. 'There is more than one way to "kill" the Bible', he says. 'You can dissect it, analyze it, abstract it. You can read its ragged stories and ragamuffin poetry, and from them you can derive neat abstractions, sterile proposi-tions, and sharp-edged principles.'[57] To the emergent people the Bible was never intended to be studied and analyzed; it was meant to be embraced as art, to be read as a story. The proof is that it is written as narrative and poetry and story. Granted much of it is in this genre but, as D. A. Carson points out, much of it is also 'law, la-ment, instruction, wisdom, ethical injunction, warning, apocalyptic imagery, letters, promises, reports, propositions, ritual, and more. The easy appeal to the overarching narrative proves immensely distortive.'[58] Regarding Scripture, Carson leaves us with a powerful warning: 'At some juncture churches have to decide whether they will, by God's grace, try to live in submission to Scripture, or try to domesticate Scripture.'[59]

Emergent Hermeneutics

With such an understanding of the Scriptures how can the emerging church claim to be in any sense devoted to the Bible? By develop-ing new hermeneutics. Hermeneutics is the science of interpretation involving rules and principles that enable us to interpret anything we read, from the newspaper to the Bible, although the word is used almost exclusively in reference to Scripture. The hermeneutic used by most of us all of the time in extrabiblical literature could be called 'normal' or 'literal'. That is, we believe that words make sense, can be understood and can communicate a message that the author wants to convey. When we read tax laws, as confusing as they might be, we approach them though normal hermeneutics believing that we can and must understand what they say. When we turn to the sports page of a newspaper and read that such-and-such team just won the championship, we naturally believe that a fact has been communicated (the team won) and that we can understand what the author of the article has said, all because we use normal hermeneutics.

But when it comes to Scripture, many are not content to use normal hermeneutics (called grammatical-historical by theologians). Rather many approaches to interpretation have been invented. We have allegorical and devotional hermeneutics which add supposed hidden meanings to words and texts, liberal hermeneutics which deny the supernatural and anything that is not politically correct at the moment, and neo-orthodox hermeneutics which say that anything that 'inspires' us is the Word of God to us.

More recently new hermeneutical approaches have been invented, each attempting, in my opinion, to circumvent the clear teaching of the Word. At least three new hermeneutics are making the rounds in emergent circles:

1) **Postmodern hermeneutics (or hermeneutics of suspicion):** Since postmodernism is laced with deconstructionism, and since the emergent church is the postmodern church, it is only natural that a postmodern hermeneutic of Scripture would be developed and employed in this movement. McLaren explains it well, 'The Bible requires human interpretation, which was [is] a problem... How do "I" know the Bible is always right? And if "I" am sophisticated enough to realize that I know nothing of the Bible without my own involvement via interpretation... What good is it, liberals would ask conservatives, to have an inerrant Bible if you have no inerrant interpretations?...'[60]

I trust these abbreviated quotes express the postmodern approach to Scripture. Even if they feign belief in an inspired, inerrant Bible, it is of little consequence because we lack inerrant interpreters. In the emerging church's view, the Bible may very well be communication of truth from God to man, but since we are incapable of interpreting the Scriptures 'truthfully' it matters little.

Of course, employing postmodern hermeneutics renders the Scriptures impotent, and causes us to ask why God bothered at all trying to communicate with mankind? And what did God mean in Psalm 19 when he tells us of the benefits and power of the Word? And why did Paul tell Timothy to preach the Word (2 Tim. 4:2) if there is nothing in the Word that can be taught with confidence?

While we will agree that infallible and inerrant interpreters are non-existent, it does not follow that the Bible cannot be understood, rather the vast majority of the Scriptures are clear and comprehensible.

2) **Rhetorical hermeneutics:** McLaren defines this as,

> An approach to Scripture that among other things tells us that we normally pay too much attention to what the writers are saying and not enough to what they are doing. Rhetorical interpretation would ask, 'What is Jesus trying to do by using the language of hell?...'[61]

In other words, since we can't understand words, by postmodern necessity we are free to ignore words and try to interpret actions. This is hardly a step in the right direction as anyone who tries to interpret body language could testify.

3) **Redemptive Hermeneutics:** This is a methodology invented by Dallas Theological Seminary graduate William Webb and endorsed by Dallas professors such as Darrell L. Bock and Stephen R. Spencer, originally in order to provide some kind of justification of the egalitarian movement. Unlike many egalitarians, Webb concedes that, if the Bible is read using normal hermeneutics, men and women are given different roles and functions in the home and in the church. Webb's solution is to move beyond the written words to the spirit of the words which will allow accommodation for the views and attitudes of our age. 'While Scripture had a positive influence in its time, we should take that redemptive spirit and move to an even better, more fully-realized ethic today.'[62] Why is this important? Because 'Christians have to reevaluate their beliefs due to changing attitudes toward women and toward homosexuals.'[63]

McLaren uses this hermeneutic to teach that the Holy Spirit will continue to lead us to new truth beyond the written word. 'I can't see church history in any other way, except this: *semper reformanda*, continually being lead and taught and guided by the

Spirit into new truth.'[64] Bell uses the same hermeneutic to make this comment on Matthew 16:19 and 18:18, '[Jesus] is giving his followers the authority to make *new* interpretations of the Bible' (emphasis his).[65] These new interpretations lead to a new church, 'It is our turn to step up and take responsibility for who the church is going to be for a new generation. It is our turn to redefine and reshape and dream it all up again.'[66] But they are wrong. It is not up to us to redefine, reshape and dream up the church again; God has already settled this matter.

What these new hermeneutics have in common is the deliberate movement away from the words and message of Scripture to a new message beyond the pages of the Word. In the process, the Bible becomes nothing more than a shell or perhaps a museum piece to be admired but ignored. Scripture as handed down by God has been replaced with the imaginations of man in order to fit more succinctly with our culture. But if we have no authoritative word from God, with what is the church left? Nothing but mystery and mysticism.

Mystery

The emerging church is not excited about truth (as a matter of fact staying true to their postmodern roots, they reject and are suspicious of truth claims) but they are enamored with mystery. Donald Miller writes his book *Blue Like Jazz* to develop this very theme. He summarizes his thoughts,

> At the end of the day, when I am lying in bed and I know the chances of any of our theology being exactly right are a million to one, I need to know that God has things figured out, that if my math is wrong we are still going to be okay. And wonder is that feeling we get when we let go of our silly answers, our mapped out rules that we want God to follow. I don't think there is any better worship than wonder.[67]

When Rob Bell is faced with giving answers to the pertinent issues of life such as heaven, hell, suicide, the devil and God or love and rape, he has no answers — just hugs. 'Most of my responses were about how we need others to carry our burdens and how our real needs in life are not for more information but for loving community with other people on the journey.'[68] But the classic answer belongs to McLaren, who virtually closes his book *A Generous Orthodoxy* with this statement:

> Consider for a minute what it would mean to get the glory of God finally and fully right in your thinking or to get a fully formed opinion of God's goodness or holiness. Then I think you'll feel the irony: *all these years of pursuing orthodoxy ended up like this – in front of all this glory understanding nothing* (emphasis his).[69]

There we have it. Ultimately, we know nothing. Even though Jesus was clear that we worship God in spirit and in truth (John 4:23), in the emergent church there is no truth, no theology, no understanding of God. However, this does not stop them from embracing the presence of God or so we are told. How does such a 'faith' survive? On the basis of mysticism.

Mysticism

Peter Rollins, emergent leader with Ikon in Northern Ireland, says, 'We at Ikon are developing a theology which derives from the mystics, a theology without theology to complement our religion without religion.'[70] Emergent leaders can say such things because of their overbearing emphasis on experience. Kimble has it backwards when he asserts, 'The old paradigm taught that if you had the right teaching, you will experience God. The new paradigm says that if you experience God, you will have the right teaching.'[71] Sanctus1, an emerging church in England, says it well, 'We… believe that God is not defined by theology… Experience is vital and experience defines us.'[72]

Carson is correct, 'For almost everyone within the movement, this works out in an emphasis on feeling and affections over against linear thought and rationality, on experience over against truth.'[73] The emerging church is a movement in search of an experience, not the truth. They seem to have little realization that an experience based on anything but truth is a mirage. The Scriptures never deny the proper place of experience, but our Lord says, 'You will know the truth and the truth will make you free' (John 8:32). The emergent church is a movement that is in bondage to its own imagination, not one held captive to the truth of God.

Conclusion

There is an old story of an elderly man driving his pickup truck through the countryside. Beside him, but hugging the door on the passenger side, was his equally elderly wife. They have been married for fifty years and, while still devoted to one another, their love had lost most of its romance. They lived together comfortably but the passion was little more than a memory.

On this particular day they happened to cross paths with another pickup, this one occupied by a young couple. As is often the case with young lovers, the young woman was sitting as closely as possible to her man. The older woman watched them for a few moments and finally said to her husband, 'Why don't we sit close any more?'

The old gentleman stewed over the question for a few moments then finally proclaimed, 'It ain't me that moved.'

He has a good point, one that is applicable to the church today. If many evangelical churches now maintain a different position than ascribed in Scripture, there can be no question about who has moved. By the same token many other churches have 'stayed home', continuing their faithful relationship with their Lord and his Word.

As I conclude this book I feel a bit like Jude must have felt. Jude sat down to write a little epistle about 'our common salvation' (v. 3a), but then felt the necessity to write a letter 'appealing that you contend earnestly for the faith which was once and for all handed down to the saints' (v. 3b). Why the change in plans? Because 'certain persons have crept in unnoticed' (v. 4).

Similarly, I sat down to write a more 'positive' sequel to my book *This Little Church Went to Market.* I wanted to address God's instructions and mandates to his church (which I did in chapters nine through eleven). And I wanted to frame this in the context of our postmodern times (which I did in chapters one through five).

But I cannot resist discussing and warning about those who have 'crept in unnoticed'. 'Creep' is an interesting word. It describes an animal or person who is attempting to enter some forbidden place. A fox creeps into the henhouse because if detected he will be killed. A spy infiltrates (creeps into) the enemy's camp to learn forbidden secrets. So false teachers penetrate evangelical ranks in stealth-like fashion in order to destroy the faith.

There is a difference, however. Whereas the fox knows what he is trying to devour, and the spy is following a careful plan of espionage, the false teacher most likely does not recognize himself as such. Do the seeker-sensitive icons, the emergent church leaders or the mystics identify themselves as the target of Jude's warning? Highly unlikely. Instead these individuals view themselves as those who would rescue the church. They see the people of God as floundering spiritually, without direction or purpose, devoid of intimacy with Christ, morally unchanged and hopelessly out of step with the times. Someone needs to lead the church out of this quagmire and into what God intended. So the false teachers do not see themselves as harming the body of Christ, but as delivering it.

Many of those, maybe most, who have crept in, have pure motives but their template is wrong. They want to advance God's people to the next level but their plans are drawn from the wrong sources. While giving much lip-service to Scripture, the fact is they have abandoned God's truth for the wisdom of men. They have appointed themselves as the shepherds of men's souls but they do not know God's Word. As a result, our times resemble those of Jeremiah's when the Lord said, 'My people have become lost sheep; their shepherds have led them astray' (Jer. 50:6).

These false shepherds have been able to gain traction within the evangelical community because there exists a famine of the Word among God's people. Solid exposition of Scripture has long since vanished from most pulpits. We are reminded of Ezekiel 34:26, 'Woe, shepherds of Israel who have been feeding themselves. Should not shepherds feed the flock?' This is arguably the most biblically illiterate generation in the West since before the Reformation. As such it is ripe for deception. False teachers and teachings are able to creep in 'unnoticed' because few have enough biblical knowledge and discernment to detect error.

This situation is not only unfortunate, it is disastrous. Peter warned, 'But false prophets also arose among the people, just as there will be false teachers among you, who will secretly introduce destructive heresies' (2 Peter 2:1). The only safeguard we have against 'destructive heresies' is a thorough knowledge of the Word of God. This is the direction Jude points us. 'But you beloved, ought to remember the words that were spoken beforehand by the apostles of our Lord Jesus Christ' (v. 17).

The church today needs the type of shepherds God promised Israel. 'Then I will give you shepherds after My own heart, who will feed you on knowledge and understanding' (Jer. 3:15). These are men who know the Word and passionately proclaim it. And the church needs Christians who hunger and thirst for God's truth, a people who cry out, 'Give us the Word!'

Contrary to what the doubters proclaim, God has many who have not bowed the knee to the latest fad or trendy teaching. These are Christians who passionately love God and His Word, who believe it pleases the Lord to 'contend earnestly for the faith' (Jude 3), who are confident that God has and will continue to build His church, who take the worship of their Lord seriously, who joy in telling the unbeliever of Christ's saving grace and sharing the 'old, old story' with their brothers and sisters. These represent the church which has stayed home with its Saviour, tethered to him by the Word, rather than chasing after every 'wind of doctrine' and 'deceitful scheme'. May their tribe increase and may this book help them to do so.

Appendix

Barna's Revolution

With all the winds of change, doctrinal corruption, errant movements and 'conversations' buffeting the church of Christ, what is next? Some believe that the next wave will be the abandonment of the local church. Some are even calling for that abandonment, claiming that the local church has lost its influence in society as well as its power to transform lives. The local church is ready for the trash heap. What is needed instead is not the local church at all but some alternative forms. These forms, we are assured, will lead to a new revolution of God's people. Leading the charge toward this new 'revolution' is none other than George Barna, the famous evangelical founder of The Barna Group, a research organization which for years has led the Christian community through its marketing studies and opinion polls.

Before we get ahead of ourselves I am reminded of a popular but chubby Christian author who, some years ago, wrote a book on how to lose weight. The uniqueness of this situation was that the author had been on his diet only for a short time and had not reached his targeted weight. Still, so dramatic had been his weight loss that he rushed to inform the rest of the world about his method. But, as almost anyone knows who has ever gone on a diet, it is relatively easy to lose weight, even in large amounts, at the beginning, only to gain it back in due time. Our author thought he had discovered the wave of the future in weight management and was eager to share his finding — but, alas, he was premature.

Not only did his waistline 're-expand', but his regimen has also long since been forgotten.

All of this reminds me of George Barna's belief that he has caught the wave of the future concerning the church. Within twenty years, he confidently predicts, the local church will lose 50 percent of its adherents to alternative forms.[1] The fulfilment of this prediction is inevitable, according to Barna, because he has observed the new 'spiritual diet' program of Christians and has determined they will continue on the regimen. This is the case even though Barna admits that these 'mini-movements' are small, disorganized, inadequately led and lack a strategic framework. But not to worry, these signs of weakness are actually evidence that God is behind it all.[2] I am reminded of a Yogi-ism, 'Prediction is very hard, especially about the future.'

Barna believes a revolution has begun which is 'an unprecedented reengineering of America's faith dimension that is likely to be the most significant transition in the religious landscape that you will ever experience.'[3] He sees this revolution as a 'viable alternative' to the local church.[4] And he considers himself a participant in the revolution.[5] As a matter of fact, as his book *Revolution*, which details his predictions, progresses, the reader begins to realise that Barna is the revolution's head cheerleader and chief source (he lists his organization as the only resource regarding the revolution).[6]

So what do we learn about the revolution in Barna's book? Not much. Barna is long on hype and hyperbole and pitifully short on details. Not a single quote from a participant in the revolution is given. Not a footnote. Not the name of one individual or organization. Not one verifiable stance on doctrine or philosophy of ministry. Rather we are inundated with generalities from unknown sources about nebulous beliefs and practices. Still, we are to believe Barna because his 'research' supposedly backs his claims. If this is any indication of the kind of research the Barna Group does it should give us real pause before we accept its reports at face value.

Nevertheless, based almost entirely on anecdotal accounts, Barna predicts (with complete confidence) that the local church is facing a decline of mammoth proportions. Those leaving the local church are not doing so because of their own spiritual lethargy, but because they recognize the impotence of the church and want something more, something better. While constantly bashing the local church in *Revolution*, Barna holds up the revolutionists as model Christians. Although at one point he seems to indicate that there are a dozen 'mini-movements' each having less than three million adherents,[7] he is never specific enough about these 'mini-movements' to even evaluate his statistics. Describing these 'millions' of widely-diverse people, he writes, 'It is comprised of a demographically diverse group of people who are determined to let nothing stand in the way of an authentic and genuine experience with God... They are God-lovers and joyfully obedient servants. They are willing to do whatever it takes to draw closer to God.'[8]

To Barna, the revolutionaries are a breed of super-saints who have rediscovered what the church lost somewhere along the way. This might be a good time to note that Barna (and his revolutionaries) are largely reacting to the market-driven, seeker-sensitive church that he helped create. Having formed the consumer church (largely through his surveys that revealed to church leaders what people wanted), he now recognizes that this church has lost its spirit. It has been gutted of its transforming power because, for over two decades, the paradigm has been to give people what they think they want rather than what God says they need. Is it any marvel then, as the shine fades from this new model, that people begin to realize they have bought a lemon? Of course Barna is disappointed with the consumer church; it has been constructed from the surveys, opinion polls, and felt-need blueprints drawn up in Barna's own workshop. The local church is now flush with drama, entertainment, social events, psychology and programs galore, but is absent the power and glory of God. All of this was predictable. When we abandon God's blueprint we are left with those concocted by men — men like Barna.

Now Barna has changed direction, recognizing the church model he helped engineer has a fatal flaw. He is declaring a recall. Bring in your old model, he is saying, and we will give you a new one — one that works. But before we exchange the keys we might want to remember what Barna delivered last time. When we are sold a lemon, we are wise to tread lightly before we go back to the same dealer. Maybe we should look around first. And maybe we should consult the original Engineer as to what He had in mind in the first place. The solution to the seeker-sensitive church that Barna built is not to trash the local church but to return to the biblical model.

This brings us to another vital deficiency of *Revolution*. The book has virtually no interaction with Scripture. It is astounding that a Christian leader wants to lead a revolution without careful analysis of the biblical text. Yes, he does make an anaemic attempt to cite a few Scripture references (e.g. pp. 20–22), but he carefully avoids any discussion of God's design for the local church complete with elders, deacons, church discipline, body life, instructions to teach, care for souls, etc. Where is Barna's analysis of 1 Timothy 3, Titus 1, Acts 20, Hebrews 13, Ephesians 4:11–16, 1 Corinthians 12–14, Revelation 2-3 and numerous other passages? Rather than thoughtful discussion of Scripture, Barna reacts with scorn to anyone who dares to challenge his unbiblical position, painting him as confrontational.[9]

Even Barna's research has serious and obvious flaws. He sees the church as ineffective, lacking in cultural and spiritual power. His surveys indicate that there is no substantial difference in the way Christians and unbelievers live. He asks, 'If the local church is God's answer to our spiritual needs, then why are most churched Christians so spiritually immature and desperate?'[10]

Good question, but before we get too excited we should look behind the scenes at the Barna Group's assumptions while taking these surveys. Many have long recognized that Barna is far too generous with his definition of who is a Christian or an evangelical. Some, including myself, believe that if you take Barna's numbers and divide them by three you will come closer to the truth. Why? Barna's seeker-sensitive movement (his earlier model) has flooded the local church with tares. I am convinced many 'evangelical' churches today are comprised largely of unbelievers. These are individuals who would claim to be born again or even evangelical for survey purposes, but who do not know Christ. Even by Barna's own minimalist definition of a biblical worldview, he identifies only nine percent of evangelicals having one. If 40 percent of Americans claim to be born again (according to Barna) but only nine percent of those have a biblical worldview, something is amiss in the foundational definitions. By earlier standards a true Christian would by necessity have a biblical worldview. A little calculation then would tell us that nine percent of 40 brings us to about 3.6 percent. In other words, the believing community in America may be closer to 3.6 percent than to 40 percent.

If this is the case in America, perhaps the most religious nation in the Western world, think about the dismal spiritual state of other nations. One study in 2000 showed that while 48% of people in the United Kingdom claimed to belong to some religious organization (as compared to 86% in America), only 7.5% actually attended church (any church) on an average Sunday.[11] That is down from 10% in 1989 and 12% in 1979.[12] There is a virtual freefall of interest in Christianity in the UK, yet 71% still call themselves "Christians".'[13]

I suggest that if Barna would take his surveys from those who truly represent biblical Christianity, his findings would be radically different. Instead Barna has an incredibly wide definition base. He provides a chart in *Revolution* stating that 70 percent of Americans rely upon a local church for their spiritual experience and expression.[14] That will change to 30-35 percent by the year 2025 as half the church members exit local congregations. But in that 70 percent figure Barna has lumped together liberal, cultic, nominal attendees, Catholics, Protestants, etc. The figure has no substantial meaning, especially in light of the fact that more reliable figures tell us only about 35 percent of Americans attend church services now on any given weekend. My point is this: Barna throws all those claiming any church affiliation into one giant pot, then comes up with the conclusion that the church has failed to produce spiritually alive Christians. I say he needs to survey another pot. Examine those churches that have stayed with God's plan, that have faithfully taught the Word, practiced church discipline, evangelized with the biblical gospel message, worshipped with God as the focus, and majored on the majors of Scripture. I think you will find those churches producing spiritual, passionate believers. And, since that is true, rather than jettisoning God's plan and replacing it with another corrupt rendition we should recommend that the local church return to the Bible for the divine blueprint.

This option is not a real one for Barna. Barna is convinced that the revolution is from God[15] and we 'cannot fight God and win'.[16] We therefore are not to judge or even discern this movement; rather we need to jump on board.[17] Whether the revolution meets the test of Scripture is not important to Barna. God is doing a new thing and we better join up or be steamrolled. Resistance is futile. Fortunately Barna is not the last word on the church. God has reserved that for himself.

Notes

Preface
1. Jay Tolson, 'Forget politics. It's about the music', *U.S. News and World Report*, 19 April 2004, p.72.
2. James T. Draper, Jr. and Kenneth Keathley, *Biblical Authority* (Nashville, Tennessee: Broadman & Holman Publishers, 2001), p.73.

Chapter 1
1. Douglas Groothuis, *Truth Decay* (InterVarsity Press: Downers Grove, Ill: 2000), p.35.
2. Michael J. Kruger, 'The Sufficiency of Scripture in Apologetics', *The Master's Seminary Journal* (Vol. 12, No. 1), Spring 2001, p.71.
3. Gene Edward Veith, Jr., *Postmodern Times* (Wheaton: Crossway Books, 1994), p.27.
4. Kruger, p.72.
5. Groothuis, p.20.
6. Kruger, p.73.
7. Gerald L. Zelizer, *USA Today*, 8 January 2002, p.13A.
8. www.religioustolerance.org/uk_rel.html.
9. www.bbc.co.uk/1/hi/programmes/wtwtgod/3518375.stm.

Chapter 2
1. Jean-Paul Sartre, *Nausea* (New York, N.Y.: New Directions Publishing Corporation, 1964), pp.122, 133, 114, 112.
2. Os Guinness, *Time for Truth* (Grands Rapids, Mich.: Baker Books, 2000), p.78.
3. Mark Noll, Nathan O. Hatch, George M. Marsden, *The Search*

for Christian America (Colorado Springs: Helmers & Howard, 1989), pp.39, 87-93, 107, 130-131.

4. Mark A. Noll, *Scandal of the Evangelical Mind* (Grand Rapids/Leicester: Eerdmans and IVP, 1994), p.97.

5. Iain H. Murray, *Evangelicalism Divided* (Carlisle, Penn: The Banner of Truth Trust, 2000), p.197.

6. Michael J. Kruger, 'The Sufficiency of Scripture in Apologetics', *The Master's Seminary Journal* (Vol. 12, No. 1), Spring 2001, p.73.

7. Guinness, p.58.

8. Douglas Groothuis, *Truth Decay* (Downers Grove, Ill: InterVarsity Press, 2000), p.209.

9. Groothuis, p.210

10. For an excellent article on this subject see *Christian History* (Vol. XXI, No. 2), 'A Deadly Give and Take' pp.19-24. By Paul Crawford.

11. Gene Edward Veith, Jr., *Postmodern Times* (Wheaton, Ill.: Crossway Books, 1994), p.51.

12. Kruger, p.73.

13. Murray, p.254.

Chapter 3

1. For a more detailed study of postmodernism, I would recommend the following books: *Truth Decay* by Douglas Groothuis, *Time for Truth* by Os Guinness, *The Gagging of God* by D. A. Carson, and *Postmodern Times* by Gene Edward Veith Jr. Both Groothuis' and Veith's books deal exclusively with postmodernism, while the other two books handle other truth related subjects as well.

2. Douglas Groothuis, *Truth Decay* (Downers Grove, Ill: InterVarsity Press, 2000) p.225.

3. D. A. Carson, *The Gagging of God* (Grand Rapids, Mich.: Zondervan, 1996) p.19.

4. Carson p.45.

5. Gerald L. Zelizer, 'Quick Dose of 9-11 Religion Soothes, Doesn't Transform', *USA Today*, 8 January 2002, p.13.

6. George Barna, *The Barna Report: What Americans Believe* (Ventura, CA: Regal Books, 1991), pp.83-85, 120.

7. Gene Edward Veith, Jr., *Postmodern Times* (Wheaton: Crossway Books, 1994), p.16.
8. Veith p.180.
9. John Leo, 'Professors Who See No Evil', *U. S. News and World Report*, 22 July 2002 p.14.
10. Rick Shrader, 'Postmodernism', p.11 (an unpublished paper).

Chapter 4
1. Gene Edward Veith, Jr., *Postmodern Times* (Wheaton: Crossway Books, 1994), pp.212-213.
2. D. A. Carson, *The Gagging of God* (Grand Rapids, MI: Zondervan, 1996). p.221.
3. Douglas Groothuis, *Truth Decay* (Downers Grove, IL: InterVarsity Press: 2000), p.265.
4. Veith, pp.213, 215.
5. Groothuis, p.275.
6. Iain H. Murray, *Evangelicalism Divided* (Carlisle, Penn.: The Banner of Truth Trust, 2000), p.74.
7. Os Guinness, *Time for Truth* (Grand Rapids, MI: Baker Books, 2000), pp.78-79.
8. Monte E. Wilson, 'Church-O-Rama', *The Compromised Church*, ed. John H. Armstrong (Wheaton, IL: Crossway Books, 1998), pp.67, 68.
9. Quoted by Steve Rabey, 'This Is Not Your Boomer's Generation', *Leadership*, Fall 1996, p.17.

Chapter 5
1. Quote by Douglas Groothuis, *Truth Decay* (Downers Grove, IL: InterVarsity Press Ill: 2000), p.268.
2. Groothuis, p.21, 22.
3. Michael J. Kruger, 'The Sufficiency of Scripture in Apologetics', *The Master's Seminary Journal* (Vol. 12, No. 1), Spring 2001, pp.76-77.
4. D. A. Carson, *The Gagging of God* (Grand Rapids, MI: Zondervan, 1996). p.74.
5. Groothuis, p.188.
6. Groothuis, p.166.

Chapter 6
1. Alan Wolfe, *The Transformation of American Religion* (New York: Free Press, 2003), p.3.
2. Ibid.
3. Ibid., p.31.
4. Ibid., p.32.
5. Ibid., p.33.
6. Ibid., p.36.
7. Ibid., p.194.
8. Ibid., p.195.
9. Ibid., p.76.
10. Ibid., p.256.
11. Udo W. Middelmann, *The Market Driven Church* (Wheaton, IL: Crossway Books, 2004). p.201.

Chapter 7
1. Bruce Shelley and Marshall Shelley, *Consumer Church*, (Downers Grove, IL; InterVarsity Press , 1992), p.126.
2. Taken from Alistair Begg, What Angels Wish They Knew (Chicago,: Moody Press, 1998), pp.151-152.
3. C. H. Spurgeon, *Lectures to my Students* (Grand Rapids,: Associated Publishers and Authors, 1971), Volume 3, p.58.
4. D. A. Carson, *For the Love of God, Volume 2* (Wheaton: Crossway Books, 1998), reading for January 23.
5. John White and Ken Blue, *Healing the Wounded* (Downers Grove, Illinois: InterVarsity Press, 1985) p.34.

Chapter 8
1. Charles G. Finney, *So Great Salvation* (Grand Rapids, Michigan: Kregel Publications, 1965), p.58.
2. I am purposely avoiding saying that these people are being brought to Christ through these methodologies, for I do not know that is the case. However, they have been brought into membership or attendance of a local church by certain enticements, whether biblical ones or not.
3. D. A. Carson, *The Gagging of God* (Grand Rapids, Michigan: Zondervan, 1996), p.30.
4. Robert Schuller, *Self-Esteem: The New Reformation* (Waco,

Texas: Word, 1982), p.64.

5. Donald E. Green, 'The Folly of the Cross', *The Master's Seminary Journal* (Volume 15, No. 1), 2004, p.62.

6. Ibid., p.64.

7. Ibid., p.65.

8. Ibid., p.66.

9. Ibid., p.68.

Chapter 11

1. James T. Draper Jr. & Kenneth Keathley, *Biblical Authority* (Nashville: Broadman & Holman Publishers, 2001) pp.2-3.

2. William James, *The Varieties of Religious Experiences* (New York: Longmans, Green, and Co., 1922) p.91.

3. Tom Ehrich, "Fear-based Faith Helps No One," (Springfield, IL: *The State Journal Register*, 22 May 2005) p.15.

4. John MacArthur, *Why One Way?* (Word Publishing Group, 2002) pp.47-48.

5. See my book, *This Little Church Went to Market*.

6. J. P.Moreland, *Love Your God with All Your Mind* (Colorado Springs: NavPress, 1997) p.19.

7. Don Kistler, General Editor, *Sola Scriptura!* Michael Horton, Forward (Soli Deo Gloria Publications, 2000) p.XV.

8. Quoted by Douglas Groothuis, *Truth Decay* (Downers Grove, IL: InterVarsity Press, 2000) p.265.

9. Ibid.

10. Ibid.

Chapter 12

1. John MacArthur, *Reckless Faith*, (Wheaton, IL: Crossway Books, 1994), p.27.

2. Brian Moynahan, *The Faith,* (New York: Doubleday, 2002), p.269.

3. Georgia Harkness, *Mysticism*, (Nashville, Tennessee: Abingdon Press, 1973), p.19.

4. Winfried Corduan, *Mysticism: an Evangelical Option*, (Grand Rapids: Zondervan, 1991), p.32.

5. See Corduan, pp.45-46.

6. William James, *The Variety of Religious Experiences*, (New York:

Longmans, Green and Co. 1922), pp.377-429.
7. Moynahan, p.270.
8. Harkness, p.32.
9. Corduan, p.35.
10. Moynahan, p.270 and Harkness, p.39 (Bernard also considered the 'kisses of the feet' in The Song as picturing the purgative stage and the 'kisses of the hand' as the illuminative p.91).
11. Harkness, pp.26-27.
12. William Johnston, *The Inner Eye of Love: Mysticism and Religion*, (Collins/Fount, 1981), p.127.
13. Georgia Harkness, *Mysticism* (Nashville, Tennessee: Abingdon Press, 1973), p.106.
14. See Winfried Corduan, *Mysticism: an Evangelical Option?*, (Grand Rapids: Zondervan, 1991), pp.106-107.
15. See Ray Yungen, *A Time of Departing,* (Silverton, Oregon: Lighthouse Trails Publishing Company, 2002), p.75.
16. Richard Foster and Emilie Griffen, *Spiritual Classics*, (San Francisco: Harper, 2000), p.17.
17. As cited in Yungen p.75.
18. Thomas Merton, *Conjectures of a Guilty Bystander, Image Edition of 1989*, (Garden City, NY: Doubleday, 1966), pp.157, 158.
19. Richard Foster, *Celebration of Discipline*, Third Edition, (San Francisco: Harper, 1978), p.149.
20. Ibid., p.150.

Chapter 13
1. Georgia Harkness, *Mysticism*, (Nashville, Tennessee: Abingdon Press, 1973), p.25.
2. Richard Foster, *Celebration of Discipline*, (New York: HarperCollins, 1998), p.19.
3. Ibid., p.25.
4. Ibid., p.96.
5. Ibid., p.102.
6. Ibid., p.25.
7. Ibid., p.166.
8. Cited in James Sundquist, *Who's Driving the Purpose Driven Church?*, (Bethany, OK: Rock Salt Publishing, 2004), p.93.
9. Richard Foster, p.28.

10. Cited in Ray Yunger, *A Time of Departing*, (Silverton, Oregon: Lighthouse Trails, 2002), p.84.

11. Richard Foster, p.15.

12. Ibid., p.107.

13. Winfried Corduan, *Mysticism, an Evangelical Option?*, (Grand Rapids, Michigan: Zondervan, 1991), p.120.

14. Richard Foster, p.17.

15. Winfried Corduan, p.138.

16. Yungen, pp.133-134.

17. Agnieszka Tennant, "The Patched Up Life and Message of Brennan Manning," *Christianity Today*, June 2004, p.42.

18. http://www.gracecathedral.org/enrichment/excerpts/exc_20010328.shtml

19. http://www.gracecathedral.org/labyrinth/

20. Ibid.

21. Ibid.

22. Steven Spearie, "A Spiritual Journey on Canvas," "*The State Journal-Register*" 16 January 2005, p.19.

23. The Berean Call, July 2004, p 6.

24. Karen Burton Mains, *Lonely No More* (Dallas: Word Publishing, 1993), Mains pp.114-115.

25. Ibid., p.123.

26. Ibid., p.124.

27. Ibid., p.124.

28. Ibid., p.115.

29. Ibid., p.71.

30. Gregory A. Boyd, *Seeing Is Believing* (Grand Rapids: Baker Books, 2004), p.12.

31. Ibid., p.196.

32. Ibid., pp.72, 86, 95, 127-128, 134, 205.

33. Ibid., pp.117-134.

34. Ibid., p.114.

35. John Weldon and John Ankerberg, "Visualization: God-Given Power or New Age Danger" Part 1, p.1.

36. David Hunt and T. A. McMahon, The *Seduction of Christianity* (Eugene, Or: Harvest House, 1984), p.124.

37. Adelaide Bry, *Visualization: Directing the Movies of Your Mind* (New York: Barnes & Noble Books, 1979), p.1

Chapter 14

1. Recognized, but not official leaders of the movement at this time include: Brian McLaren, Rob Bell, Dan Kimball, Doug Pagitt, Leonard Sweet, the late Mike Yaconelli, Spencer Burke, Erwin McManus, Tommy Kyllonen (aka Urban D), Jason Clark (in the UK) and Donald Miller. Some see Richard Foster and Dallas Willard as key mentors for the movement.

2. Some of the promoters of the emerging church include Youth Specialties, The Ooze and The Emergent Village.

3. See Andy Crouch, "The Emergent Mystique", *Christianity Today*, November, 2004, pp.36-41. This article described the excitement and chaos at the 1994 Emergent Convention in Nashville.

4. Ibid., p.39.

5. Brian McLaren, *A New Kind of Christian*, (San Francisco: Jossey-Bass, 2001), pp.19-22. In many ways the emergent church can trace its birth to the publication of this book.

6. Dan Kimball, *The Emerging Church*, (Grand Rapids: Zondervan, 2003), p.60.

7. Ibid., p.115.

8. D. A. Carson, *Becoming Conversant with the Emerging Church*, (Grand Rapids: Zondervan, 2005), p.42.

9. Kimball, p.143.

10. www.pbs,org/wnet/religionandethics/week846/interview.html

11. *Christianity Today*, p.38.

12. Ibid., p.40.

13. Brian McLaren, *A Generous Orthodoxy* (Grand Rapids: Zondervan, 2004), p.293.

14. *Christianity Today*, p.38.

15. Ibid.

16. Ibid.

17. McLaren, *A New Kind of Christian*, p 162.

18. Leonard Sweet, Andy Crouch, et al., *The Church in Emerging Culture: Five Perspectives*, Leonard Sweet, ed., (Grand Rapids: Zondervan, 2004), p.35.

19. D. A. Carson, p.84.

20. Lewis Carroll, *Alice's Adventures in Wonderland* and *Through the Looking Glass* (http://www.sabian.org/Alice/gchap06.htm).

21. Kimball, p.175.
22. McLaren's book, The *Last Word and the Word after That,* is primarily a deconstruction of the doctrine of hell.
23. Brian McLaren, *The Last Word and the Word after That*, (San Francisco: Jossey-Bass, 2005), p.134.
24. Ibid., p.XVIII.
25. McLaren, *A Generous Orthodoxy*, pp.286-287.

Chapter 15

1. Quoted by David Roach, "Leaders Call 'Emerging Church Movement' a Threat to Gospel," BP News, 23 March 2005, www.ews.net/bpnews.asp?id=20420
2. Dan Kimball, *The Emergent Church*, (Grand Rapids: Zondervan, 2003), p.178.
3. Brian McLaren, *A New Kind of Christian,* (San Francisco: Jossey-Bass, 2001), pp.xiv-xv.
4. Rob Bell, *Velvet Elvis*, (Grand Rapids, Zondervan, 2005), p.12.
5. Ibid., p.26.
6. Ibid., p.27.
7. Ibid., p.20 (cf. p.21).
8. Ibid., p.27.
9. Ibid., p.21.
10. Brian McLaren, *A Generous Orthodoxy,* (Grand Rapids, Zondervan, 2004), p.223.
11. *The Last Word and the Word after That,* p.197.
12. Kimball, p.53.
13. www. Sanctus1.co.uk/2006/01/blahmachester-pall-singh-richared.html.
14. www.greenbelt.org.uk/?a=626&pr=82.
15. Ibid.
16. McLaren, *A New Kind of Christian,* p.161.
17. McLaren, *A Generous Orthodox,* p.235.
18. Brian McLaren, *The Story We Find Ourselves In*, (San Francisco: Jossey-Bass, 2003), p.102.
19. McLaren, *A Generous Orthodoxy,* pp.195-197.
20. Al Mohler, www.crosswalk.com/news/weblogs/mohler/?adate=2/16/2005#131087
21. Brian McLaren, *The Last Word and the Word After That*, (San

Francisco: Jossey-Bass, 2003), p.xii.

22. Ibid., pp.61-64, 71-79.

23. Ibid., p.74.

24. Ibid., pp.103 (cf. pp.182-183).

25. McLaren, *A Generous Orthodoxy*, p.37.

26. McLaren, *The Last Word and the Word After That,* p.182.

27. Ibid., p.183.

28. Ibid., p.35.

29. Ibid., p.138.

30. Ibid., p.69.

31. Bell, pp.109-110.

32. McLaren, *A New Kind of Christian,* p.129.

33. Ibid., p.84.

34. Ibid., p.106.

35. McLaren, *A Generous Orthodoxy*, p.97.

36. McLaren, *The Last Word and the Word After That*, p.84.

37. Ibid., p.149. McLaren has adopted N.T. Wright's understanding of the gospel which is termed the New Perspective. The New Perspective says that we have misunderstood the New Testament and that the real issue of such books as Romans is not to explain the gospel but how to bring Jews and Gentile together in the Kingdom of God (see pp.149-153).

38. Ibid., p.153.

39. Brian McLaren, *A Generous Orthodoxy* (Grand Rapids: Zondervan, 2004), p.113.

40. Ibid.

41. Ibid., p.223, 234.

42. Ibid., p.263.

43. Ibid., p.264.

44. Rob Bell, *Velvet Elvis* (Grand Rapids: Zondervan, 2005), p.147,150

45. Dan Kimball, *The Emerging Church* (Grand Rapids: Zondervan, 2003), p.224.

46. Bell, p.165.

47. Ibid.

48. Ibid., p.167.

49. Ibid., p.166, 167.

50. Brian McLaren, *The Last Word and the Word after That* (San

Francisco: Jossey-Bass, 2005), p.111.

51. Bell, p.41.
52. Andy Crouch, "The Emergent Mystique," *Christianity Today*, November, 2004, p 38.
53. Bell, p.42.
54. McLaren, *A Generous Orthodoxy*, p.86.
55. Bell, p.68.
56. McLaren, *The Last Word*, p.111.
57. McLaren, *A New Kind of Christian,* p.158.
58. D. A. Carson, *Becoming Conversant with the Emerging Church* (Grand Rapids: Zondervan, 2005), p.164.
59. Ibid., p.172.
60. McLaren, *A Generous Orthodoxy*, pp.133-134.
61. McLaren, *The Last Word*, p.81.
62. William J. Webb*, Slaves, Women & Homosexuals: Exploring the Hermeneutics of Cultural Analysis* (Downers Grove, IL: InterVarsity, 2001), p.247.
63. Ibid., p.25.
64. McLaren, *A Generous Orthodoxy*, p.193.
65. Bell, p.50.
66. Ibid., p.164.
67. Donald Miller, *Blue Like Jazz* (Nashville: Thomas Nelson, 2003), p.206.
68. Bell, p.30.
69. McLaren, *A Generous Orthodoxy*, p.294.
70. www.emergingchurch.info/stories/cafe/peterollins
71. Kimball, p.188.
72. www.sanctus1.co.uk/whoweare.php.
73. Carson, p.29.

Appendix

1. George Barna, *Revolution* (Wheaton: Tyndale House Publishers, 2005), p.49.
2. Ibid., pp.54-55.
3. Ibid., p.vii.
4. Ibid., p.ix..
5. Ibid., p.x.
6. Ibid., p.141.

7. Ibid., p.54.
8. Ibid., pp.124-125.
9. Ibid., pp.134-135.
10. Ibid., p.30.
11. www.vexen.co.uk/religion/rib.html.
12. www.religioustolerance.org/ul_rel.html.
13. www.vexen.co.uk/religion/rib.html.
14. Ibid., p.49.
15. Ibid., pp.19, 79, 82, 139.
16. Ibid., p.137.
17. Ibid., pp.20, 127, 136, 139-140.

This little
church
WENT TO MARKET

Is the Modern Church Reaching Out or Selling Out?

The most successful arm of the evangelical church in recent years, in terms of growth, money and prestige, has been the market-driven (seeker-sensitive, new paradigm, user-friendly) church. Because of this success these churches are being mimicked all over the country, and indeed, the world. But is this church fully dressed? Is she outfitted in the biblically prescribed robes of evangelism, edification, worship and instruction? Or, is she wrapped in rags composed of empty human philosophy stitched together with bits and pieces of truth? If the latter is true, why have so few seemed to notice? It is the intent of this book to attempt to answer some of these questions.

ISBN 0 85234 596 8